Praise for *Nowhere Man*

"A new look at the last days of John Lennon..."
—*L.A. Times Bestsellers*

"Rather like re-reading a favorite detective story...though you know how the story's going to end, you still wind up willing events to unfold differently."
—David Thompson, *Mojo*

"Robert Rosen's gripping account of John Lennon's five-year seclusion in the Dakota building makes it impossible any longer to agree with the cozy popular image of him during this period as a devoted father and bread-baking, domesticated househusband. This is a portrait of...the twilight of an idol."
—Alan Jones, Editor, *Uncut* magazine

"After reading this book I felt an affinity for Lennon; his life with all of its torments, joys and pains was real to me."
—Sydney Murray, *Vision Magazine*

"A haunting biographical depiction of Lennon's final years of self-imposed seclusion and professional exile."
—Mark Wallgren, *Goldmine*

"We become privy to first-hand knowledge about Lennon's final days which has never before seen the light of day....the book makes for engrossing reading."
—Steve Wide, *Beat Magazine*

NOWHERE MAN

NOWHERE MAN

The Final Days of John Lennon

Robert Rosen

Nowhere Man: The Final Days of John Lennon
Quick American Archives
Oakland, California

Cover Illustration: Andrea Ventura
Cover Design: D-Core
Design & Composition: Melanie Haage

Photo credits:
pp. xii, 19, 22, 31, 43, 69, 89, 90, 107, 147,
160, 182, 183, 197 AP/Wide World Photos
pp. 12, 207 Marcel Miller

"Nowhere Man" editorial reprinted by permission of *The New York Post*.
Town & Country horoscopes reprinted by permission of the Patric Walker
estate.

Printed in the United States of America.

Publisher's Cataloging-in-Publication Data
(Provided by Quality Books, Inc.)

Rosen, Robert, 1952-
    Nowhere man : the final days of John Lennon / Robert
Rosen.
        p.   cm.
    Includes bibliographical references and index.
    ISBN 0-932551-51-3

    1. Lennon, John, 1940-1980--Last years. 2. Rock
musicians--Great Britain--Biography.   I. Title.

M:420/:38R67 2002   782.42166'092
                                                QB102-674

To Mary Lyn,
for being there

ACKNOWLEDGMENTS

Nowhere Man is a story that refused to die. For two decades people have kept it alive with spiritual, financial, legal, and editorial support. They are:

Victoria Looseleaf, Darius James, David Lewis, Marty Appelbaum, Jay Butterman, Jerry Rosen, Irwin Rosen, Eleanor Rosen, Karla Zounek, Sonja Wagner, Maryanne Cassata, Joyce Snyder, Rita Trieger, Paul Slimak, Byron Nilsson, Beth Rosenblum, Steve Colby, Kay Hart, Royce Flippen (for "John Lennon Diary Blues"), Alexis Lipsitz, Gail Harris, and Jamie Forbes

And especially my agent Jim Fitzgerald for finding a way

PRELUDE

John Lennon and Yoko
Ono in Denmark, 1970,
ten months after
being married on the
Rock of Gibraltar.

JOHN LENNON'S DIARIES

IVE DAYS AFTER JOHN LENNON WAS MURDERED, HIS personal assistant, Fred Seaman, a close friend, came to my apartment. He was visibly shaken, his eyes bloodshot, tears streaming down his face. There was work to be done, he said. The previous summer, during an extended stay in Bermuda, John had told him that if anything should happen to him, it was Seaman's job to write the true story of his final years. It would not be the official tale of a happy, eccentric househusband raising Sean and baking bread while Yoko ran the family business. Instead, it would be the story of a tormented superstar, a prisoner of his fame, locked in his bedroom raving about Jesus Christ, while a retinue of servants tended to his every need.

"It'll be the ultimate John Lennon biography," Seaman told me. "It's what John wants. It's our job to carry out his will."

I chose to believe him. I had no reason not to. I was a 28-year-old unemployed writer, with a master's degree in journalism, whose last occupation was cab driver. I'd known Seaman since college; I'd been his editor at the school newspaper.

Fred started working for Lennon in February 1979. After one day on the job he told me, "We must collaborate on a book."

I said yes and began taking extensive notes in my diary.

For two years we were on a magical mystery tour. When Seaman was in town, we cruised all over New York and beyond, once going as far as Montreal, in Lennon's brand-new apple-green Mercedes Benz, smoking fat spliffs of John's potent marijuana and blasting rock 'n' roll on the customized Blaupunkt sound system.

When Seaman was traveling with the Lennons or unable to get

away, he called me every week from wherever he was staying—the Dakota, Cold Spring Harbor, Palm Beach, Bermuda—and told me, in explicit detail, what was going on. It was a routine that continued for those two years.

Then, the unthinkable, recorded in my diary:

12/9/80 John Lennon was killed last night. At around 7:00 I'd smoked the last bit of dope Fred had given me, my "Lennon Dope." I looked at those crumbs in the bag and said, "What the fuck am I saving this for, sentimental reasons? This stuff is for getting stoned." It was Jim Morrison's birthday and I was listening to a Doors special on WPLJ. When news of the murder came over the radio, all I felt was a chill. Around 2 A.M. I went down to the Dakota. I felt it was important to observe the scene. I shed a few tears, I couldn't help it. God help you, John Lennon. Thank you for touching my life. At 5 A.M., when I got home, I tried to call Fred at the Dakota. I got the accountant. He said Fred wasn't available. I said, "Tell him I called and that I'm sorry." There was nothing to say then and there's nothing to say now. There is only sickness in a sick world.

Yet, as I absorbed the unfolding events, I couldn't help but consider my own role in them.

12/10/80 I'm an eyewitness to history. I would not be human if I were not fascinated by Lennon's death. My perfectly human desire is to want to be part of the scene, to be part of history. There is a possibility Fred will ask me to begin work on the book. He called this morning to say he's quitting his job at the end of the week to begin writing it. "It's what John wants," he said. "John knew he was going to die and he poured his heart out to me. He knew I was working on a book." I'm not going to ask to participate in this project. If I'm not part of it, my life will go on as it has. But if Fred does ask me, there's no way I can say no. I believe I can execute such a project in a spirit true to John Lennon's memory.

Seaman didn't quit his job. Instead, Ono promoted him to executive assistant and gave him the run of the Dakota. After deciding that my involvement was essential, he began feeding me the raw material

I needed to write the bio: unreleased audiotapes and videotapes Lennon had recorded; photographs and slides Seaman had taken over the course of the last two years; and notes Lennon had written describing Seaman's daily errands and chores.

In May 1981 Seaman gave me John Lennon's journals. He assured me that John had told him that in the event of his—John Lennon's—death, Seaman was to use any materials he needed to tell the full story of his life. It was obvious that these leather-bound *New Yorker* magazine desk diaries were the key to the project Seaman envisioned.

Still, not until Wednesday, October 21, after a number of false starts, did I begin the process of transcribing Lennon's diaries. It was exhausting work that continued unabated until the end of November. No matter how much I transcribed, there was always more; the task seemed endless. I forced myself into a routine that rarely varied: I woke up at 5 A.M., rolled out of bed and tore into the journals. Then, for the next 16 hours, fueled by coffee and amphetamines, I wrestled with Lennon's scrawls and codes and symbols. As I transcribed his words on my IBM Selectric, I said them out loud like an incantation, and I began to feel what seemed to be Lennon's energy flowing through me.

For the first time I saw what his life was really like. I was in awe of his fanatical discipline, his total commitment to the self-imposed slavery of diary keeping. I'd never seen anything like it. He got it all down—every detail, every dream, every conversation, every morsel of food he put in his mouth, the perpetual stream of consciousness. And it was all an enormous contradiction. Here was a man who aspired to be like Jesus and Gandhi as much as he craved money and carnal pleasures.

For Lennon, his journals were his religion.

The work was slow and excruciating. It felt as if I were translating a foreign language written in a different alphabet. I put so much energy into deciphering each word, and in some cases each letter, that I had no idea what he'd written until I read back the entire passage; then I was able to fill in the missing words and phrases by context.

For six weeks I lived like a monk, confronting on a daily basis The Gospel According to John. To get a visceral sense of Lennon's life, I ate the foods that he ate. I fasted, starving off 12 pounds to achieve a weight of 138, close to Lennon's 135. I lived as he would have lived, but without Yoko, without Sean, without a staff of maids, cooks, governesses, chauffeurs, and other assorted servants, seers and personal assistants. I lived as he would have lived without his Beatle past, without his superstar present, without his $150,000,000. His words my only companion, I existed in virtual isolation

Then, on January 4, 1982, Ono fired Seaman. He assured me that the project would continue; he'd given John Lennon his word that he'd tell the true story. And he now had an "angel" to finance the book. All our expenses would be taken care of. Also, he said, since I'd been working so hard, it was time I took a vacation.

On February 9, 1982, I flew to Jamaica. When I returned to New York on February 27, my apartment had been ransacked. Everything I'd been working on—Lennon's diaries, the photo-copies of Lennon's diaries, the transcripts of Lennon's diaries, the manuscript, the tapes, the photos—had been taken. There was no sign of forced entry. It was Seaman; he had the keys. It was only then that I realized that virtually everything Seaman had told me about why we were doing the project was a lie.

I sank into a state of near-paralysis but managed to file a complaint with the police. A detective said there was nothing that could be done. I couldn't prove that a crime had been committed.

Lennon's diaries haunted me. I'd wake up in the morning and details would come flooding back. I began taking notes on everything I could remember. By mid-April I'd put together a manuscript that included information from the diaries and everything that had happened since the day Lennon was murdered. I thought I had the scoop of the century, a rock 'n' roll Watergate. As a journalist, I felt it was my obligation to tell the story. One of the people I sent the manuscript to was Jann Wenner, editor and publisher of *Rolling Stone*. We met in early July. He said that he believed me, but that he could do nothing with my manuscript because I had no proof. He needed time to think. We met again later in the week. He'd spoken with Ono. She was unaware that any diaries were missing. I had only one choice, said Wenner: "Tell your story to Yoko Ono. I want to save your karma."

On August 16 I went to the Dakota to meet with Ono's companion, Sam Havadtoy, and Ono's lawyers. I told them everything I knew, and that I feared for my life. They put me in a hotel under an assumed name.

A month later I met with Ono herself.

_9/13/82_ 4:13 P.M. _We were in Studio One, sitting on her couch, beneath the ceiling painted like the sky. I was leaning against an embroidered pillow that said, "A woman's place is in the House and Senate." She was taking notes._

"We need to clear this up before Mercury Retrograde begins," I told her.

She agreed, and asked me when that was.

"September 19th."

"Then we have to work fast," she replied, and asked me if I knew about any other deals Seaman had been making.

I said no.

She squeezed my arm. "He was working for the financier for a year before you knew about it, darling. John wanted to fire Fred for using the Mercedes. He knew about cars. He kept track of the mileage, you know."

I told her everything that had happened since 1979, when they hired Seaman. It just poured out of me, as it always does.

When I finished, she said, "We're in this together, you know. I want you to cooperate with us in an investigation."

"I am cooperating. That's why I'm here."

She asked to read my personal diaries, which Seaman had not taken. "There may be things in there that not even you understand."

I said okay. "It's only fair. After all, I read John's diaries."

"You shouldn't have read them." She looked at me harshly. "John's diaries are so sacred I don't even want to read them."

"Why don't you just hire me and let me help you from the inside."

She cracked a smile. "We'll call it an 'advance' on your book."

I went into the bathroom with Sam. We stood on opposite sides of the toilet, negotiating. He agreed to give me $200 per week plus an additional $300 on the first of each month. He then pulled a wad of bills from his pocket and peeled off two crisp hundreds.

The next day I loaned Ono 16 volumes of my journals, about a half-million words. They covered more than three years, from the day Seaman was hired through the day I left for Jamaica. We sat together in her kitchen—me, Ono, Havadtoy—reading the diaries together. Ono used the information in them to have Seaman arrested and to get back her possessions. Seaman pleaded guilty to grand larceny and was sentenced to five years' probation.

For 18 years I was unable to get my diaries back; I thought I'd never see them again. I was in no position to fight. I wanted peace, and I took the advice of John's songs—I surrendered, I let it go. Then, just as the first edition of *Nowhere Man* was going to press, Ono returned my diaries.

Nowhere Man is a work of both investigative journalism and imagination. I have used my memory of Lennon's diaries, as well as notes written in 1982 when I originally re-created the diaries, as a roadmap to the truth. But I have used no material from the diaries.

To put this book together, I've taken information gleaned from Lennon's music; his published writings and interviews; the historical record; my own observations of the scene inside his home and office in the Dakota; and informal conversations that I had with his staff, business associates, family members, and friends. These people include Yoko Ono, Sean Lennon, Julian Lennon, May Pang, Neil Aspinall, Elliot Mintz, Fred Seaman, Helen Seaman, Norman Seaman, Rich Martello, Greg Martello, and Sam Havadtoy. At the time I was speaking with them, neither they nor I had any idea that what they were telling me would be used in a book. But as a matter of habit, I took notes in my diary on all the conversations.

I've also retraced Lennon's steps through Liverpool, London, New York, Palm Beach, and Bermuda. I've correlated the chronology of Lennon's final years with the zodiac and Mercury Retrograde charts, because the Lennons ran their lives by the zodiac and Mercury Retrograde charts. I've studied the raw materials that filtered daily through Lennon's mind: horoscopes from *Town & Country* magazine; editorials from *The New York Post*; science stories from *The New York Times*; gossip from *The National Enquirer*; numerology from *Cheiro's Book of Numbers*; books about tarot, astrology, magic; and the literature of Henry Miller and Hunter S. Thompson.

In rare instances vital information, such as the details of Lennon's dreams, could neither be extrapolated from the public record nor found in an independent source. In those cases, I've used my imagination as best I could to recreate the texture and flavor of Lennon's life.

The result of this confluence of information, imagination and intuition is the story of what it was like to be John Lennon.

J E R U S A L E M :
A   F A N T A S Y

YOKO, ON THE ADVICE OF HER COUNCIL OF SEERS, SENT *John on another directional voyage to Jerusalem.*

"*Time has stood still for two thousand years,*" *Lennon wrote, looking out his hotel window at the Jaffa Gate, the walls of the Old City.*

Inside the walls, he wandered the streets, the Via Dolorosa, hiding behind sunglasses, his shoulder-length hair flowing like Jesus' underneath a Panama hat. He gawked at the Arabs in their headdresses, sitting on stools outside ancient coffeehouses, smoking huge chunks of hashish, three or four of them pulling off enormous hookahs, like Alice in Wonderland. He, too, wanted to smoke but he was afraid. Don't want to do time in an Israeli prison, he thought. Child beggars, their eyes infected by disease, swarmed around him, demanding money. He gave them his coins. Everywhere he went, he felt the energy of Jesus Fucking Christ, Abraham and Mohammed, like they walked here an hour ago....

On the third day he took a cab to the Mount of Olives, Gethsemane: "A Mercedes driven by a Jew in Jerusalem takes me to The Garden of Jesus' agony." In the garden he got down on his knees and prayed, "Dear God please forgive my sins...."

He wept.

I can feel Jesus' pain, he thought. I, too, will be betrayed.

A young woman, an American tourist, asked if he was okay. He invited her back to his hotel, and it was only after he'd taken off his hat and sunglasses that she realized who he was.

"*Oh my God,*" *she said. "Nobody's going to believe this....I picked up John Lennon in Gethsemane.*"

"*I want to wash your feet,*" *he told her.*

She said, "Yes."

He filled a basin with water. She sat in a chair. He got down on his knees...took off her sandals...sponged the dust from her feet. "I'm your humble servant," he said.

She looked at him, her eyes filled with fear and astonishment.

"This is what I must do," he explained.

PART I

DAKOTA

1980

Marcel Miller

In 1973, John Lennon and Yoko Ono moved into the Dakota, 1 West 72nd Street, across the street from Central Park.

BEING RICH

"If I hadn't made money honestly, I'd have been a criminal. I was just born to be rich."

NEW YORK CITY, WEDNESDAY, JANUARY 9, 12:06 P.M. —The words astounded John Lennon as he stared at the caption beneath the old photograph of himself in *The National Enquirer*. He remembered thinking them but had no recollection of ever saying them out loud. Though he loved reading about himself in the tabloids, he hadn't spoken to a reporter in five years. He hated the motherfuckers. Since he'd gone into seclusion, virtually everything they wrote about him was libelous fantasy. But there was nothing he could do about it. He was fair game. It had been open season on Lennon for 18 years. Still, he had to admit, it was flattering that the press couldn't get along without him and Yoko.

At the advanced age of 39, he was mellowing, learning a bit of self-control. He no longer screamed primally when he came upon a fabricated "exclusive" written by a hack he'd never met, claiming that John Lennon had gone bald or completely insane.

But this nameless *Enquirer* reporter was clearly not a person to be trifled with. *Does he have psychic powers? Can he read my mind? Is he with the CIA? Is my phone tapped again? Is there an internal security leak? Did Yoko tell him? Is it done by satellite? What else do they know?*

So taken by the quotation was Lennon that he clipped it and pasted it on the first page of his 1980 *New Yorker* magazine desk diary.

Something was terribly wrong with John Lennon and his wife, Yoko Ono, as the new decade dawned on the Dakota. Their lives were falling apart. John's annual prayer for the continued enjoyment of his health and wealth had apparently fallen upon deaf ears. The situation had become so desperate that servants speculated among themselves about the possibility of a double suicide. But that was mostly wishful thinking. Suicide was out of the question. There was at least one thing John was sure of: he did not want his son Sean to grow up an orphan. And he believed deeply in the existence of God. If he killed himself, there'd be a terrible karmic price to pay. But mostly, a double suicide would make too many of the wrong people rich.

The strain of a life gone out of control showed in Yoko's face. One month short of 47, she was beginning to look like an old woman. Menopause loomed. Gofers were routinely dispatched to Europe to import large quantities of hormonal rejuvenation pills and creams unavailable in the United States. *Stay young at any cost. Money is no object. Ignore the fact that the odds of ever being a rock star in your own right have gone from slim to nil.*

Acute depression hung in the air and it showed in John's writing. Since retiring from the music business in late 1975, after Sean was born, he compulsively poured all his creative energies into keeping diaries.

His journals were his life. They gave him something constructive to do with his time; they kept him sane. They were his best friend, his only companion. The writing had always been fragmented, but now it bordered on the incoherent. These days, every word was agony. John knew his self-imposed five-year tenure as "househusband" was coming to an end. He no longer wanted to be like the *New Yorker* cartoon that showed a man with a guitar lying on the couch while in the next room his wife tells her friend, "He's being de-hyped." It was time to get back into gear—"centered," he called it. It was time to face the world again.

But there had not been a moment's peace since the new year began. The Dakota was a madhouse, overrun by staff, friends, family, and the workmen who were building a new playroom for Sean. One morning the superintendent was summoned to exterminate an enormous waterbug that John had found in the bathroom but refused to kill.

Yoko's mother, Isoko Ono, whom everyone called Baba, was in from Japan, and neither John nor Yoko wanted to deal with her. They foisted her off on a servant, who chauffeured her around town in a Mercedes-Benz station wagon. But Baba was having a great time. Her favorite activity: eating lunch at Howard Johnson's in Times Square.

For no good reason at all, John woke up one morning that first week in January feeling euphoric. Thinking about Yoko's mother gave him the urge to call his aunt, Mimi Smith. On impulse, he invited her to move to America and live at the Dakota.

Mimi, who had taken John in when he was six months old, was living in the town of Poole in Dorset, in southwest England, in a seaside bungalow that John had bought for her in 1965, after Beatles fans had laid siege to Mendips, her old Liverpool home.

"John," she said, "I'm happy here. I don't like America."

"But you've never been to America, Mimi...and there's plenty of room here."

Moments after he hung up the telephone he wondered if he'd gone mad. He couldn't believe he'd just invited Mimi to move in. *What if she changes her mind and says yes?*

Lashing out at everybody around him, John felt his mood nose-dive into despair and self-reproach. He was certain that the problem was in the stars and turned to Patric Walker's horoscope in *Town & Country* magazine.

Since 1970, when the British astrologer had accurately predicted that John would soon leave England permanently, Lennon had been convinced that Walker's horoscopes were the most precise ones available anywhere. Every month he clipped Libra for himself and Aquarius for Yoko. Underlining significant passages, he correlated them with upcoming events, scribbling notes of warning or things to look forward to. At the end of the month, he reviewed his findings. Never did he declare the horoscope itself inaccurate. The only inaccuracies were in his interpretations. This month, as usual, Walker was dead on the money.

"Librans," he wrote, "don't seem to like January." *(No fucking shit!!!)* "And the astrological reason is that this is always a time when the Sun in Capricorn brings family disputes and difficulties to a head." But, with the sun "beautifully aspected by Jupiter, Mars and

Saturn in Virgo," there was hope for the year. "A force within you enables you to remove any obstacles in your path."

John hoped Walker was right about the force within.

Yoko's horoscope pointed out that "friends have been responsible for a great many of your recent misfortunes."

Elliot Mintz, a tiny man with a propensity for wearing white suits, had been staying at the Dakota since Christmas; it was the Lennons' holiday tradition to have him as a guest. The former radio DJ and TV news reporter was one of the few people both John and Yoko trusted implicitly. He'd grown friendly with Yoko in 1972, after conducting a remarkably positive television interview. Now he was a devoted friend and servant—a *troubleshooter*. Whatever needed to be done, Elliot did, professionally and without question.

John thought about Christmas Eve, which he'd spent with Mintz in their private English gentlemen's salon, "Club Dakota." John, dressed formally in tails and his old Quarry Bank brown and yellow school tie, played the Yamaha electric piano Yoko had given him and sang duets with Elliot. Then the two men danced around the room, playing rock 'n' roll records on Sean's antique Wurlitzer jukebox.

But by the end of the week John had had more than enough of Elliot and told him to go home. He hadn't even given him a Christmas present.

Then things quieted down a bit, and Lennon was finally able to spend an entire day alone and undisturbed. He received a letter in the mail from Nicky Hopkins. Hopkins, who'd worked with John in 1968, playing electric piano on *Revolution,* and later on the *Imagine* sessions, said that he needed work badly.

He can go fuck himself, John thought, tossing the letter in the trash. The last time they worked together Hopkins' ego was out of control. He was playing too many mind games.

Lennon's mood was momentarily boosted when he received an invitation for a party that Greta Garbo and the Sheik of Saudi Arabia were both scheduled to attend. But Yoko said they couldn't go—it was out of the question. The numbers and the stars weren't right, particularly for her. It was going to be a traumatic February because of an eclipsed moon in her birth sign.

Retreating to his bedroom on the seventh floor, John rolled a thick joint of potent Thai weed and lit it up. *Thai one on,* he thought as he sat in bed sulking. He stared at the faces on the silent TV, flipping through the channels with the remote control until he grew groggy and faded to sleep.

THAT MAGIC FEELING

SOMETIMES JOHN'S DAY BEGAN AS EARLY AS 4 A.M. Refreshed from a deep, sound sleep, he'd sit up in bed and immediately record the exact time. Then he'd walk across the room to the window seat and, looking out at Central Park and midtown Manhattan, wait for dawn. Or he'd go back to sleep and have another dream.

Usually, though, he woke up around six or seven. His biological clock was finely tuned. Provided there were no major disruptions, his time of awakening didn't vary by more than two or three minutes for months at a time. Since there was never any real reason to wake up, he never set the alarm. It was a morning routine more akin to chronic unemployment than independent wealth—a magical feeling, nothing to do, *nowhere to go...nowhere to go...*

He'd then take stock of his state of mind, which generally fell into one of three categories: Up, Okay, or Down. When he'd smoked too much marijuana the night before, he awoke feeling groggy. Overeating just before going to sleep, which he often did after smoking too much Thai weed, gave him indigestion. And on those rare occasions when his willpower broke down completely and he drank a glass of wine or beer with dinner, he was invariably shocked to wake up hungover. It was the price he paid for an alcohol-sodden youth. Anything he imbibed, even in the smallest quantity, gave him a hangover.

If John's energy level and ambition were running high, a half hour or more of yoga was next on the agenda. Introduced to yoga in 1967 by Maharishi Mahesh Yogi, the founder of Transcendental Meditation, he'd continued to practice it over the years. It cleared his mind, relaxed him. Outside of walking, yoga was the only exercise he ever did. But spiritual rather than physical reasons motivated him to continue meditating.

AP/Wide World Photos

The Beatles arrive in Wales during August 1967
to study yoga and meditation with the Maharishi
Mahesh Yogi (center). (From left: John Lennon,
Paul McCartney, Ringo Starr and George
Harrison.) In his ongoing quest for spiritual
perfection, Lennon tried to meditate for a half
hour every morning during the Dakota years.

Yoga had taught him discipline, helped him in his constant battle to keep his primal urges under control. And those urges had to
be controlled if he was ever to realize his greatest ambition—to
achieve a state of spiritual perfection by following The Way of The
Masters: Jesus, Buddha, Mohammed, Krishna and Gandhi. Yoga
was one method of attaining this perfection. There were other ben-
efits, too. John believed that if he meditated long and hard enough,
he'd merge with God and acquire psychic powers, like clairvoyance
and the ability to fly through the air. And he wanted those powers
as badly as he wanted anything. Yoko also wanted him to have

them, and she urged him to keep meditating. Clairvoyance, she pointed out, would be the ultimate money-making tool.

The path to perfection was long and arduous; it took a lifetime of dedication and meditation, not to mention a pure heart. A half hour of sitting in the "bogus" position every morning was not going to bring John enlightenment and he knew it. He no longer had the willpower to meditate for eight consecutive hours as he'd done 12 years ago at the Maharishi's ashram in Rishikesh, India. But in his most optimistic, euphoric moods, he thought there was still a chance that the *kundalani* energy would shoot up his spine and that he'd levitate off the ground, at last becoming one with God.

Optimism, energy, and ambition, however, were not running high in early 1980. John was slipping backwards; he'd strayed from The Path and often wondered if he'd ever be able to follow it again. Morning yoga sessions were becoming progressively infrequent. He was giving in to his primal urges. He was smoking too many "ciggies" and too much Thai. He was drinking too much coffee and eating too much food.

Once he had done yoga virtually every day. Now entire yoga-less weeks slipped by. He chastised himself for his lack of discipline. Yoga made him feel good and he couldn't explain why he no longer did it. Then he pushed the thoughts out of his mind. The chastising stopped. He was learning to accept his vices again.

But no matter how lazy he got, he was always vigilant about his weight. During his five years of seclusion, the maintenance of a stable weight was the one area of discipline that never broke down. He'd never forgotten that during his Beatle days and the first years of marriage to Yoko, he had a visible potbelly. He hated that part of himself, saw himself during those years as an "overweight junkie." Hanging around the house all day, he knew how easily the pounds could creep back on. Fear of fat haunted him.

John, who was about 5'10", weighed himself every morning on one of two scales—"machines," he called them—which gave him two different readings. Over the past five years his weight had ranged between 135 and 140 pounds, usually closer to 135—slim by anyone's standards. But when he approached 140, he'd freak, and a day-long fast was the usual course of action. If he felt the situation was particularly critical, he'd embark on a week-long juice fast. Watching the pounds melt away filled him with joy. He felt as if he were in control. Sometimes, though, he drank so much juice that he put on weight. The only time the scale ever nosed over 140 pounds was during a juice fast.

"Fucking juice is making me fat!!!" he thought.

For five years barely a week went by when John didn't fast or attempt to fast. Usually he'd begin a day-long fast, but by dinner time his willpower would break down and he'd gorge himself on junk food, stuffing into his mouth anything that happened to be in the refrigerator. Then he'd call himself a fool. The next day he'd try to fast again and the same thing would happen. By the end of the week, he'd have attempted seven fasts and broken all seven. But by holding himself to one feeding frenzy per day, he was still able to get his weight back down to 135.

John's physical appearance, too, was in a state of constant flux. He made a point of never looking exactly the same for two consecutive days. As a matter of survival, he didn't want to be too recognizable. This was easily accomplished by hiding behind a wide variety of hats, sunglasses, and clothing—"masks" he called them. Only the "Troupies" (formerly known as "Apple Scruffs"), the hard-core Lennon watchers who camped out in front of the Dakota, wouldn't be fooled by the costume changes. But he could achieve a tolerable level of anonymity while walking the streets of Manhattan. That was why he lived there.

He considered himself a chameleon. For purely artistic reasons, he enjoyed tinkering with his hair and beard, just to see how many different looks he could manage. He had talented hormones and could grow a respectable full beard in a month. When it became too easy to spot the bearded Lennon, he'd shave it off. When he got sick of shaving every morning, he'd grow it back. He was in a perpetual beard/beardless cycle.

Just after turning 39, in November 1979, John began growing what was to be his last beard. By early 1980 it was in full bloom and he liked it. His hair was getting really long, too; it fell to his shoulders. He hadn't cut it in over six months. Sometimes he'd hide his hair under a wide-brimmed hat. Other times he'd wear it in a ponytail, which came in two varieties: regular, which hung down his

John Lennon continues to play his guitar as a fan grabs him onstage in Rome, June 1965. Such over-exuberance made Lennon wary. Even years after Beatlemania, while living in New York, he was hesitant to walk outside without disguising himself.

neck, and samurai, which was actually more of a bun that stuck up in the air. When he wore it samurai-style, even his face looked Asian.

John had mixed feelings about his hair. It was an on again/off again love affair. He'd go for weeks ignoring it, letting the dandruff and grease build up to alarming levels. Then he'd wake up one morning and decide he loved his hair again. He'd begin taking meticulous care of it, washing it in macrobiotic shampoos, conditioning it with expensive oils and creams.

He'd let his hair grow long and unmanageable only because he hated going to barbers. He didn't trust them. Even the "celebrity" barbers tended to be overwhelmed by him. They seemed more concerned with getting an autograph than concentrating on the job. He was afraid they'd butcher him with some bizarre styling, then write an article about it for the *Enquirer*. It was a real problem. John lost sleep when he had an appointment with a barber. Once he mentioned to David Bowie that he wanted to take a haircut but didn't know where to go. Bowie recommended his personal stylist and set up an appointment for him. The day of the haircut, John worked himself into a state of acute anxiety. Then, much to his amazement and relief, he got a haircut he was happy with.

After showering and choosing a hairstyle each day, it was time to get dressed. Assuming he wasn't setting foot outside the Dakota, which was usually the case, John would put on jeans and a T-shirt or polo shirt. His favorite T-shirt was red and emblazoned with The Great Seal of the United States, the Freemason's symbol found on the backs of dollar bills and on the signs in front of psychic parlors. He loved the magical "floating eye" pyramid.

If John wanted to go out, he'd first check with "Mother." Yoko almost always woke up before him, usually around five o'clock. She didn't need much sleep. Normally, she stayed downstairs in her office, Studio One, most of the night, napping fitfully on the couch and making business calls to Europe and Japan or plotting her next move with her tarot card reader and business advisor, Charlie Swan, whom John called "The Oracle," or simply "O." If Yoko was not at her desk when John woke up in the morning, he knew that she was downtown, in Soho, meeting with the O.

S E A N

JOHN POKED HIS HEAD INTO SEAN'S ROOM AND STOOD IN the doorway watching him sleep. Tears welled in his eyes. Sean looked so peaceful. Even after four years, John still couldn't believe he really had a son like Sean. As long as Sean was okay, it didn't matter what else happened. Every day was a miracle.

He was glad that Sean had finally found the courage to sleep alone in his room—at least most of the time. Though he'd still occasionally demand that his governess sleep with him, it was a vast improvement over the way things used to be. Sean hated being alone, especially at night. Until he was three, he slept in bed with John and Yoko. They loved it. It was more togetherness than they'd ever known. But they also knew that it wasn't a good idea to be sleeping with a three-year-old boy every night. John wanted Sean to learn to be a man.

Sean often awoke with a smile. John would kiss him and they'd go to the kitchen for breakfast.

Sean was the best thing that had ever happened to John. In Sean he saw a last-chance opportunity to repent for all his past sins against family. John had never completely reconciled his guilt over the way he'd deserted his first wife, Cynthia, and their son, Julian—whom he hadn't really wanted—for Yoko. Nor had he ever fully exorcised his pain and anger over the way his own mother, Julia, and his father, Freddy, had deserted him as a child. Sean had the power to make John whole again. John's greatest fear was that he'd grow distant from Sean and lose him permanently, as he'd lost everybody he'd ever loved. Sean was the only thing that meant more to John than money. Without Sean, even money would be meaningless.

From the time Sean was two years old, John began to treat him as an equal. With each passing day, it became increasingly clear that in Sean, he had a genius on his hands. Sean was beginning to show signs of grasping difficult philosophical concepts about God, life, and death.

"Life's a crock of shit," Sean had once told him. "But you have to keep trying."

At times it was as if John forgot he was dealing with a baby. If they had a fight, John sulked until Sean forgave him.

John did everything in his power to give Sean the security he'd never known as a child. Consequently, Sean was spoiled rotten. He had no sense of reality. John was King, Yoko was Queen, Sean was Prince. And when Sean gave orders, the servants jumped. He got what he wanted when he wanted it. If he didn't, he screamed—and didn't stop screaming till he got it. Just like his daddy, Sean had little primals, which the servants called tantrums.

Sean had already been around the world. When he got tired of hanging around the Dakota, he could go with his nanny to the Lennon estate on Long Island. He always stayed up as late as he wanted. If he didn't want to, he wouldn't have to go to school next year. It never occurred to him that it was not like this for most four-year-old children. Sean simply accepted being surrounded by a wide variety of very interesting people who paid constant attention to him 24 hours a day. Naturally, Sean loved this attention and could never get enough. Should it momentarily stop, he'd primal till it started again.

Sean understood that his father used to be a Beatle and to have been a Beatle was something very special. But Sean did not fully grasp that the reason people treated him the way they did was because he was sole heir to the Lenono fortune—or misfortune, as the servants preferred to call it. The only thing Sean knew about money was that he always had it.

"Money grows on the Lenono tree," he'd heard people say, and there was, in fact, a money tree, said to have the power to sprout banknotes, that Yoko kept inside a "magical" pyramid in the room in which she kept her collection of pyramids.

THE LUNATIC INCIDENT

IF ANYTHING EVER HAPPENED TO JOHN, HE WANTED SEAN to have written documentation of the fact that he was the most significant part of his life. He wanted Sean to understand how much he loved him and how often he thought about him.

On the day of a total solar eclipse in 1979, John composed for Sean a message of eternal love that was meant to be read after John was dead. Hoping that it would help Sean to remember the day, John drew a picture of the eclipse—a big black circle that looked like an ovum as seen under a microscope.

John did everything he could to chronicle in uninhibited detail the first five years of Sean's life. Someday, John thought, Sean will be able to relive those years as if watching a movie. Some of the most intimate moments of Sean's life were documented with Polaroid pictures.

John kept track of every time that Sean threw up and agonized over every one of his childhood diseases. Once Sean had a seriously infected mastoid. John had to take him to the hospital. There was a slim chance, the doctor said, that Sean's hearing might be permanently damaged. John took Sean home and began a prayer vigil, begging God every day to please let his son recover. By the end of the week, Sean had fully recovered, and John wept.

From the day Sean was born, there was always a great fear of kidnapping, and John immediately began taking precautions. If nobody knew what Sean looked like, he'd be that much more difficult to kidnap, so John was perpetually vigilant about paparazzi. For the first five years, not one clear photograph of Sean appeared in the media.

Still, there were numerous kidnapping threats, most of them by cranks. One morning in late 1977, just before Christmas, John answered the phone.

"Unless you give me $250,000 cash," said a man with a heavy Spanish accent, "I'm going to kidnap Sean and kill you and your wife."

John tried to shrug it off. Fearing publicity, he didn't call the police. He didn't even mention it to Yoko. But the next day, the man, who became known as the Latin Lunatic, called again and sounded very serious. John was shaking as he hung up the phone. He knew he had no choice but to contact the FBI.

Two agents arrived at the Dakota within the hour. They were polite, reassuring. The only way to handle it, they told John, was to monitor the phone calls and stake out the building. John, Yoko and Sean were not to set foot outside. John gave the agents permission to do whatever was necessary.

The phone calls continued, but the Latin Lunatic always hung up before the agents were able to trace them. Time was growing short, he warned John, leaving explicit instructions about where and when to leave the money. "Don't call the police," he said.

John felt helpless. He'd been getting the phone calls daily, sometimes twice a day, for a week, and there was nothing the FBI could do. He couldn't stand being cooped up in the house anymore. He needed to go Christmas shopping. Then, on the ninth day, the calls stopped. The Latin Lunatic was never heard from again. The FBI agents left, assuring John that it was now safe to go outside. But it was months before John's nerves settled down. Every time the phone rang, he jumped out of his skin.

ANSWERED PRAYERS

SEAN WAS FOREVER PUSHING JOHN AND TESTING HIS limits. There were no limits, it seemed. The more he pushed, the more he got away with.

Sometimes Sean's behavior infuriated John, but he didn't know what to do about it except to tell Sean to apologize. Sean was stubborn and he hated to apologize for anything. John's idea of discipline was to send Sean to his room. Intellectually, Sean understood that John was angry at him and that being sent to his room was something called "punishment." But the idea of being locked in his bedroom with half the inventory of FAO Schwartz, a well-stocked jukebox, a color television, a Sony Betamax and an extensive video library—which included *Yellow Submarine, Help!* and *A Hard Day's Night*—did not strike terror in his heart. Sean would stay in his room for 20 minutes, then come out and say, "I'm sorry." That was all John wanted. Everything was forgiven.

John spanked Sean only once, when he was three years old. It happened over a bath. Sean had promised to take one, but then changed his mind and had a little primal. John grabbed him, put him over his knee and gave him a couple of whacks. Sean stopped screaming and looked at John with utter astonishment. He couldn't believe his father had hit him. But he took his bath without so much as another squawk. Then he came out of the bathroom, ran to John, hugged him and fell asleep in his arms. This, John thought, was a gift from heaven, and he thanked God for it: *Thank You. Thank You. Thank You.*

No matter how outrageous Sean's behavior, John found it impossible to stay angry at him. His love for Sean was all-consuming. Sean was a miracle. John had prayed to God for one more chance, and Sean was the answer to those prayers, proof-positive of God's existence.

Before Sean's birth, John and Yoko had been told by countless doctors that it was physically impossible for them to have more children. John had destroyed his sperm with narcotics and alcohol, they said. Yoko, who had a history of abortions, had already miscarried three of John's children.

"Give up," the doctors smugly counseled, propelling John and Yoko into a severe depression. To kill their pain they began taking heroin again, then methadone. They fled New York, driving cross-country to San Francisco. There they met with Dr. Hong, a 95-year-old Chinese herbalist, acupuncturist and recovered opium addict. First the doctor weaned them off methadone. Then he said, "You want baby? Stop taking drugs. Eat good food. In one year you will have it. I promise you." He gave Yoko a special herbal potion.

John went off the deep end in L.A.—his notorious 18-month bacchanal—but Yoko obeyed the doctor. Three years passed. Then, to their mutual astonishment, in March 1975, Yoko, at the age of 42, discovered she was one month pregnant.

The next seven months were an exercise in anxiety. Wanting to be in top physical condition when the baby was born, John worked off his tension by swimming laps in the pool at the West Side YMCA and by taking sailing trips to Long Island and Martha's Vineyard.

In May a short novel, *Skywriting by Word of Mouth (A Novelty in 4/4 Time)* poured from him. One character was named Sean. There was no story line. In a style perhaps best described as James Joyce meets Woody Allen, he filled 96 pages of Apple Corps stationary with puns, jokes, wordplay and philosophy: "If you can manicure a cat, why can't you caticure a man?" And, "You will embrace the muse, but will not be arrested."

The book originally began with a series of bogus titles concerning housewives, children, and God, which were deleted upon posthumous publication in 1986.

In the opening sentence, John described his current situation: "In which our hero finds himself, ten years later, older, madder, but definitely CURED, picketing the heinous hierarchy for custody of his soul (his organ marked accordingly)."

This was followed by a dense, Joycean paragraph that editorial wisdom again saw fit to cut.

Pounding daily on a Brother typewriter, letting off steam, John completed the manuscript in less than a month. The result was a gripping and thought-provoking book. But as soon as he finished it, he disowned it. He knew nobody would ever understand it. The idea of having to deal with editors gave him nightmares. The book business was nastier than the record business, he thought. It would be harder to publish an avant-garde novel than put out any kind of LP. It didn't even matter that those little jokey volumes he'd written over ten years ago, *In His Own Write* and *A Spaniard in the Works,* were bestsellers. Convinced that editors would torture him before agreeing to publish *Skywriting*—if they did agree to publish it—he decided he had neither the energy nor desire to fight. So he put the manuscript in his desk drawer and forgot about it. All he wanted was his baby.

In early October, the doctors, expecting complications, checked Yoko into a private room at New York Hospital—the same room in which Jackie Kennedy had given birth to Caroline. John moved into the room with Yoko, staying there around the clock. He slept on the floor, next to her bed, just as he'd done in 1968 when Yoko suffered her first miscarriage. John had recorded the child's last heartbeats with a stethoscopic microphone as it died in her womb—a sound later included on Yoko's album *Life with the Lions.* The baby, John Ono Lennon II, old enough to warrant a death certificate, was buried in a tiny coffin.

Now, seven years later, John sat by the window in the hospital room, watching sailboats on the East River and drawing in his notebook. It was the last moment of tranquility he'd know for a year.

Sean's birth by Caesarean—on John's thirty-fifth birthday, October 9, 1975, at 2:07 A.M.—rendered John ecstatic; he had no words. Sean Ono Lennon was a healthy and perfect baby. He weighed eight pounds, ten ounces.

Then the bottom fell out. The hours following Sean's birth were the most traumatic of John's adult life. The doctors accused John and Yoko of being unfit parents. Yoko was having convulsions, and it appeared as if she were going through heroin withdrawal. They could not permit a junkie to take home a baby.

John thought the doctors were mad and diabolical. He couldn't believe what was happening. First they said he couldn't

AP/Wide World Photos

John Lennon and Yoko Ono greet Yoko's
first child, Kyoko, at London Airport,
May 1969. Three years later Kyoko
would be kidnapped by her father,
Tony Cox, and Yoko wouldn't see her
daughter again until 2001.

have a baby; now that he had one, they wanted to take him away.
He wasn't going to let it happen. Sean would give him the one
thing he wanted—a real family. Why could he never have a family?
Every time he had one, he either destroyed it or someone took it
away from him. His father, Freddy, deserted him. His mother, Julia,
gave him away to his Aunt Mimi and Uncle George. He grew close
to George, and George dropped dead from a heart attack. And just
as he was getting close to his mother, she was killed in a traffic accident, run down in the street by a drunken cop.

Then there was Yoko, whose parents, descendants of Japanese
royalty, had disowned her when, at 23, she went against their will

and married a struggling musician. Her only child, Kyoko, four months younger than John's son Julian, was kidnapped in 1972 by her second husband, Tony Cox, after Yoko was awarded custody. She hadn't seen Kyoko in four years, and not until Christmas 1977 would a meeting even be attempted. The telephone negotiations would drag on for weeks. The tension would cause Yoko to teeter on the verge of a breakdown. Then, on the day of the meeting, she'd sit in the Dakota waiting for her daughter. But Kyoko would never come, and Yoko would spiral into a state of profound despair.

Now she was lying in a hospital bed, possibly near death, oblivious to everything.

John knew Yoko was not going through heroin withdrawal. As it turned out, she was having a bad reaction to a sedative. John, out of his mind with grief and rage, was ready to strangle the doctor who asked for his autograph.

John remained by Yoko's side until she recovered, feeding Sean almost every time. He loved being a daddy.

By the end of the week, they were home with their new baby. But the experience had left John shattered. For the next two months, his written vocabulary was reduced to one word: *BABY*.

Distracted by Sean and immigration problems, John virtually stopped keeping a journal in 1976. Instead of using a *New Yorker* desk diary, he wrote and drew in a little, blue, college-style composition book that he inserted in the middle of his 1975 diary. More telling than what he wrote about in 1976 were the cataclysmic events that passed without mention.

January: Mal Evans, former Beatles road manager and confidante, was shot to death—while drunk and brandishing a gun—in a Hollywood motel by the L.A. police.

February: John's Capitol Records contract expired—no more "Capitol Punishment." For the first time in 15 years, John wasn't obligated to produce music for a corporation.

April: Freddy Lennon, his father, whom he hadn't seen since October 1970, died. There were reports of father and son reconciling during a deathbed telephone conversation, but if this did occur, John did not record it in his diary.

Then, in the spring and early summer, as Yoko stayed in New York hustling up celebrities like Norman Mailer and Cardinal

Cushing to testify as character witnesses for John's upcoming immigration hearings, John retreated to the South Shore of Long Island to relax with Sean. The threat of deportation had been hanging over his head for four traumatic years because of a 1968 marijuana conviction in England that the Nixon administration had used to brand him an "undesirable alien." But if he was thinking of this, he didn't express it. He sketched sailboats and the ocean, and meditated, conjuring his past lives. He saw himself as a caveman seated at a fire, a Viking on a ship, a medieval knight. He was certain these were not dreams or hallucinations but true visions.

Then it was time for the immigration hearings. On July 27 his application for a visa was approved, the decision apparently clinched by Sean's birth nine months earlier; the government was not going to break up a family. John was amazed that the Irish justice voted against him and the Jew voted for him. He vowed to plant a tree in Israel.

John received his green card and was finally a permanent United States resident. Should he choose to return to England, where he hadn't been since 1971, or should Yoko deem it necessary to adjust his karma by sending him on a directional voyage to a distant country, he'd be allowed to reenter America.

As his retirement from the music business officially began, there was not one word about it in the diary.

Words would not flow again till 1977. And not until late that year would he attempt to describe the days and months following Sean's birth. But the pain lingered and he still couldn't do it.

COLD TURKEY

SOMETIMES IN THE MORNING JOHN COOKED BREAKFAST for himself and Sean. Scrambled eggs, vegetarian sausage, hot cereal and shredded wheat were all standard fare. Usually, though, Uda-San, a matronly servant Yoko had hired away from Tokyo's exclusive Okura Hotel, did the cooking.

John would sit in a canvas director's chair at the kitchen table, smoking his first *Gitane* of the day, sipping his first cup of coffee. Addicted to nicotine and caffeine, he'd smoke and drink nonstop, every cup of coffee inflaming his urge for another cigarette, every cigarette making him crave more coffee.

He needed the "ciggies" to curb his appetite. He needed the "café" to maintain his energy level. And he hated himself for this drug dependency. In a perpetual state of self-chastisement, for six years he prayed to God for the willpower to stop smoking cigarettes and drinking coffee. It came in flashes. Every few months he found the strength to stop everything cold turkey, vowing with all his heart and soul to give them up forever. But sometimes he couldn't even hold out for a full day. The cravings were overpowering.

Tobacco withdrawal was emotional agony, making his nerves so raw that when Uda-San said "Good morning," he'd scream, "Just leave me the fuck alone!" Everything he did, from reading the newspaper to taking a shit, made him want a cigarette. Every waking hour it was all he could think about.

Then there was the perpetual hunger. He couldn't stop eating. And there was always the need to smoke *something*...so he chain-smoked weed—which made him hungrier.

Caffeine withdrawal was even worse; it gave him blistering headaches. To kill the pain he'd drink a mug of Morning Thunder herbal tea, which actually has more caffeine than coffee. Even then the pain didn't stop, and he couldn't understand why.

Occasionally, the desire to give up coffee would slip from his consciousness for months at a time. But the urge to quit smoking rarely strayed from his thoughts. At times, he geared his entire life to quitting. In June 1978, he decided that his New Year's resolution for 1979 would be to give up cigarettes. In October, he began counting down the days to the end of the year. Then he began drawing warning signs to remind himself that he had only seven weeks to stop smoking. By December the warning signs became NO SMOKING signs with happy faces. He managed to quit smoking for the first two weeks of the new year. But by the third week he was back on cigarettes. By the fourth week he was chain-smoking again, calling himself a fool, and wondering why he didn't have the willpower to quit permanently. He was furious at himself, embarrassed by his weaknesses. Then, two months later he tried to quit again. It was another endless cycle. In early 1980 he was allowing himself to enjoy his morning cigarette and coffee with minimal self-flagellation.

MACROBIOTIC
PERFECTION

LIKE EVERYTHING IN JOHN'S LIFE, HIS DIET WAS A paradox. There could never be a happy medium. He had an insatiable sweet tooth. His favorite lunch was apple pie with a scoop of vanilla ice cream and then a salad to push it through—the European way. Yet, he tried to vigilantly maintain a perfect macrobiotic regime, keeping written track of every morsel of food he put in his mouth.

He was always conscious of the fact that he was now paying the price for having abused his body with alcohol and amphetamines for too many years. Macrobiotic food was yet another path to redemption. With carefully detailed shopping lists that left nothing to chance or the imagination, he dispatched his servants daily to New York City's best health food stores, like Tillie's in the East Village. They bought vegetables, brown rice, couscous, limited quantities of eggs, and fresh organic free-range chickens, which Yoko would sometimes use to prepare John's favorite dinner, a macrobiotic dish he called *Chicken Teri-Yoko.*

After two weeks of strict macrobiotic meals, John's willpower would break down completely. It usually happened at night after smoking some Thai weed. He'd get the munchies and gorge himself on a half-dozen big homemade cookies or a cream-filled pastry. He loved cakes, cookies, pies, custard, ice cream and chocolate but believed sugar was a poison that clogged his vital organs. He feared that if he ate enough of it he'd go insane. But he couldn't control his appetite for Thai weed either, and sometimes after a smoke, his craving for sweets drove him into the street. He'd fall into La Fortuna, a café two blocks away. He felt comfortable there, drinking endless cups of cappuccino and eating canolies by scooping out the filling.

But in the morning, after a night of bad dreams, he'd wake up in a fog, unable to focus his thoughts, racked with guilt, suffering from indigestion and diarrhea and burning with a desire to fast. Then he'd curse himself and ask *Why?* But he never had an answer.

THE SERVANT
PROBLEM

IN 1980, UDA-SAN, THE COOK AND MAID, AFTER A YEAR OF faithful service, sensed that the end of her Dakota days was near. She welcomed it. John and Yoko's unreasonable demands for perfection were getting on her nerves. She dared to question their wisdom and think for herself. These outbursts of disobedience enraged the Lennons.

The breaking point was Sean's diet. John gave Uda-San explicit written instructions on what Sean was to eat and not eat. Following these instructions wouldn't have been a problem if Sean had been cooperative. But every now and then—not surprising for a four-year-old—he'd get sick of eating brown rice and vegetables. Sometimes he'd demand a pizza pie, or ask Uda-San to cook him a hamburger, or—God forbid—insist upon eating at McDonald's. When Uda thought she could get away with any of this, she did it. Lately, though, John had been growing suspicious. One time he'd caught her red-handed feeding Sean a cheeseburger. He communicated his anger with a detailed memorandum.

John was furious because Sean was getting fat, and sometimes there was snot on his nose, too. And despite a thousand warnings, Uda continued to feed Sean the junk foods Lennon had forbidden her to bring into the house: White eggs from the supermarket! Entenmann's cakes! Frozen pizza! Meat! He didn't have the time or energy to monitor every scrap of food she purchased. If she wanted to eat crap on her own time, he didn't care. But if she couldn't obey orders, then she would no longer be permitted to work for him.

John hated to see anybody get fired, particularly someone like Uda-San. Though strong-willed and insubordinate, she could still be trusted more than most. She was not the type to write a book.

Her English, though better than rudimentary, was hardly fluent. There was a lot she didn't understand.

John was forever complaining about the disobedience of Uda-San and the other servants. He lost sleep agonizing over what to do about it. But he never actually fired anyone. That was Yoko's job.

The locks on the various apartments, offices, and storerooms were always being changed. One way people realized they were out of a job was that they didn't get the new key. The unfortunate servant or staff member would simply vanish. Uda-San would disappear at the end of the summer.

The hiring procedure at the Dakota was at best erratic and at worst incomprehensible. People were hired and fired based on the findings of the tarot card reader, Charlie Swan; the Council of Seers, an assortment of freelance astrologers, psychics and directionalists; and Yoko's own consultations with the zodiac and Book of Numbers.

It was not unheard-of for an emotionally disturbed person to be taken into the fold. One employee was fired for secretly writing to members of Congress on Lenono stationary, signing John and Yoko's names.

Yet a fan hanging out in front of the Dakota whose wildest fantasy was to get John's autograph was as likely to be hired as a professional servant who came highly recommended through the Lennons' most trusted business associates. This led to friction among the staff. Those with impeccable breeding and credentials hated the "fans who got lucky."

Rich and Greg Martello got lucky. They were teenage brothers from Queens, Beatle fanatics of the first magnitude. (One of them bore a slight resemblance to George Harrison.) Somehow, they managed to sneak into the Dakota and ambush John in the hallway outside his apartment. They asked for his autograph, and he put them both on staff as personal assistants.

Not counting the psychics, at any given time there were about a dozen full-time servants on the payroll—governesses and assistant governesses; cooks and housekeepers; a man named Mohammed who crawled around all day on his hands and knees polishing the floors; a gardener called "Tree" who tended to the houseplants, including the money tree; a gaggle of gofers to dispatch in the evening to retrieve sushi and sashimi; and an assortment of administrative and personal assistants. Most of them held the status of a useful piece of machinery, and the turnover among them was high; it was rare for anybody to last more than three years. John and Yoko's primary servant rule: Let nobody become indispensable. If anybody becomes indispensable, fire them.

Sean's governess, 60-year-old Helen Seaman, was the only exception to the rule. John actually liked her; in 1976 she'd led a campaign to petition the government to grant John permanent resident status. He enjoyed talking "at" Helen, and even mentioned her by name in his posthumously published story *The Ballad of John and Yoko*—an unheard-of honor for a servant.

Helen and her husband, Norman, an impresario who had produced Ono's performance pieces in Carnegie Recital Hall when she was a struggling avant-garde artist newly arrived in New York, had been close to Yoko for 20 years. Sean loved Helen like a mother, and she worshiped the ground on which he walked, meeting all his demands and never losing her patience or temper. She was Sean's best friend, often sleeping in his room with him.

Every time Yoko fired Helen for being indispensable, Sean primaled till he got her back. She was locked in an endless cycle of being fired and rehired.

It was also impossible to overlook the fact that if anything were to happen to John and Yoko, Helen would most likely move to legally adopt Sean. Though the will named Yoko's interior decorator, Sam Green, as Sean's guardian, Sean was not close to him. (Before the will was updated on November 12, 1979, Sean was to live in Japan with Yoko's family, whom he barely knew.) Sean would want to be with Helen, and he was strong-willed enough to get his way. With Sean would come the $150 million Lenono fortune, and even somebody as saintly as Helen had to be aware of that much money.

Unable to function without servants, John and Yoko had no choice but to trust everybody they hired—and hope for the best. In many cases, particularly with fans hired off the street, this strategy actually worked. Overwhelmed by their amazing good luck, these fans-turned-personal assistants would never dream of doing anything to violate John and Yoko's trust.

The professional servants were different. They generally felt overworked and underpaid. It's not as if they were being paid badly. Some were making as much as $36,000 per year. It was just that they were surrounded by seemingly unlimited material wealth and had countless opportunities to steal it. Over the long haul, only the more saintly servants were able to resist the temptation to steal from John and Yoko.

In the Dakota alone, along with their sprawling living quarters, office, and spare guest apartment, John and Yoko had two large basement storerooms and two entire apartments used exclusively for storage. Warehoused in these 28 rooms were expensive clothing, electronic and stereo equipment, musical instruments, art and antiques, and file cabinets overflowing with disorganized papers and correspondence going back to John's Beatle days. They never used the stuff; they just accumulated it.

John was always drawing little cartoons on scraps of paper. He'd leave them lying around the house. Some servants would steal them and sell them at Beatles conventions. Then, when the next convention came to town, Yoko would dispatch a gofer to buy up all the Lennon memorabilia in sight, including the little cartoons the other servant (since fired) had sold at the previous convention. It would all be stored and forgotten about.

John and Yoko had so many different possessions in so many different houses, rooms and vaults, it was impossible to keep track of everything. In most cases, when something was stolen they didn't even realize it. At best, the number of people with access to the most valuable art and antiques was limited.

Basically, anybody who worked for John and Yoko for an extended length of time was going to make money off them in one way or another. It was unavoidable, and John found it demoralizing. "He's ripping me off!" he'd cry out time and again in reference to some larcenous servant.

The more brazen thieves walked off with stereo components and color TV sets. Once, a housekeeper helped herself to several thousand dollars worth of Yoko's furs, then quit. The loss wasn't detected for two weeks. Then the police were called in, but nothing could be proven and the matter was dropped.

John and Yoko knew that just about everybody stole something from them, even if it was only food from the refrigerator. They accepted it as a fact of life unless it got out of hand.

John communicated with his servants by writing a profusion of detailed notes. They ranged from overtly philosophical explanations for his week-long juice fasts, to profoundly mundane macrobiotic shopping lists. These notes were so common that the less visionary gofers tossed them in the garbage after completing their errands. Other servants considered them works of art and combed through the garbage for discarded notes. Operating under the theory that any scrap of paper that John touched with a pen would someday be worth a small fortune, particularly after he was dead, they habitually collected everything they could get their hands on.

Barring a full-frontal lobotomy upon termination of employment, the worst servant problem was insoluble. John Lennon and Yoko Ono were always hot copy, and the information concerning their years of seclusion was the hottest copy of all. Lennon and Ono spawned money; industries grew up around their names. Every fact about their lives, every sentence they uttered, and every photograph taken of them had commercial value. It was a seller's market.

John understood that anybody who met him on the street or spoke to him on the telephone could turn the conversation into an exclusive for *The National Enquirer.* Anybody who actually knew him, or made love to him, and particularly anybody who worked for him, even if they were only semiliterate, could potentially get a book out of it. There was no way to legally restrict the flow of information. The Lennons were public figures, not the Pentagon. As much as they'd have liked to, they couldn't classify their lives *Top Secret: Vital to National Security. Need to Know Access Only!* Yet every servant was a potential Daniel Ellsberg, and thinking about this drove John up the wall.

The servants knew too much. A week on the job and it was obvious to anyone that reality did not match the Lennons' public image of happy but eccentric family. The longer someone worked for them, the bigger the gap grew. Should the raw truth ever become known, it would be a catastrophe.

In 1980 their tarot card reader, Charlie Swan, and their personal assistant Fred Seaman, a journalism major in college, were both secretly working on exposés, both taking extensive notes since

AP/Wide World Photos

Followed by his first wife, Cynthia Twist Lennon, and Beatles manager, Brian Epstein, John Lennon arrives for a news conference at Tickenham Studios, Middlesex, England, June 1965. John lived in fear of what Cynthia might do for revenge after he divorced her to marry Yoko Ono, but Cynthia's memoir, A Twist of Lennon, was tender and nostalgic.

day one. John suspected as much, but what was he going to do about it? Give up servants and seers? No fucking way!

Swan, after a tarot reading in which the Ten of Swords came up, had told John not to hire Seaman. The card, showing a man pierced by ten swords, was a warning of sudden misfortune, failure, pain and tears. But John disagreed.

Because the perpetuation of The Myth was an obsession, everybody who worked for John and Yoko was required to sign a confidentiality agreement that said anything they learned during their term of employment could not be used for commercial purposes. Most of the servants had neither the gumption nor the financial resources to test the validity of this "contract." Those who did discovered that for John and Yoko to enforce the agreement was difficult, time-consuming, and expensive. Still, the Lennons did everything in their considerable power to dissuade all former employees from publishing their memoirs.

Anthony Fawcett's book *John Lennon: One Day at a Time* was a diary of his three years as John and Yoko's personal assistant. The book proved to be highly complimentary, though when the Lennons learned of its imminent publication, they ordered their lawyers to block it. It couldn't be done. John was momentarily forced to resign himself to a harsh fact of the First Amendment: People cannot be stopped from publishing their memoirs.

John even tried to block the publication of his ex-wife Cynthia Twist Lennon's book, *A Twist of Lennon*. While vacationing in Japan during the summer of 1978, he learned that the book was about to come out and that excerpts would appear in London's *News of the World*. John flipped out and began frantically calling his lawyers in the United States and England. "You don't have a leg to stand on," they said.

John was despondent; Cynthia knew way too much. She'd grown up with him, witnessed his most desperate moments. He'd behaved like a bastard, in 1968 deserting her and Julian for Yoko. She'd never forgiven him and she lived for revenge. He braced himself for the worst.

As soon as the book came off the press, John had a copy delivered to him for immediate inspection. He was shocked. *A Twist of Lennon* wasn't what he expected. Cynthia's tender depiction of the early days, when they first met at the Liverpool College of Art, touched John. Misty-eyed, he sat up all night reading. He loved the nostalgia. Even the parts about Yoko, he had to admit, were fair. When he finished reading he said a prayer for his ex-wife: *Dear God, please show her The Way. Thank You. Thank You. Thank You.*

AFTER
BREAKFAST

HELEN, THE INDISPENSABLE GOVERNESS, TOOK CHARGE of Sean after breakfast. John now had the rest of the day to himself. Sometimes he went downstairs to Studio One. He liked to sit in Yoko's office and watch her in action on the telephone...and figure out whether or not she'd been snorting smack.

There had always been a special place in John and Yoko's hearts for heroin. "We were taking it in celebration," said Yoko of their heroin use in the late '60's. "We were artists. It was beautiful to be on a high." Their addictions are graphically documented in their music, the primal screams of *Cold Turkey* unambiguously communicating the agony of heroin withdrawal. But they loved the drug because nothing killed their pain better, and there was always plenty of "dirt" floating around the Dakota.

But sitting in Studio One studying Yoko, trying to determine whether she was on or off smack, had only limited entertainment value. John would soon grow bored and then might venture into the front office to check out the administrative staff.

His presence there was always disconcerting. A new employee, particularly one who'd just been hired off the street, required at least a year to get used to Lennon. The most difficult thing was learning to relax when he was in the room. The overwhelming temptation was to stare. But everybody knew that John hated being stared at and that if you stared too much, he'd complain to Yoko and she'd fire you. The best strategy was to pretend to work and try to steal looks at John's reflection in the mirror that covered an entire wall in the back of the office. If he was in a good mood and he caught you staring at him in the mirror, he'd suddenly turn around.

"Caught you looking," he'd say with a sly smile, slipping out of the room.

Usually after breakfast John wanted to be alone. He'd return to his bedroom, close the door, turn on the TV without sound. No one, not even Sean, was to disturb him for any reason. Only the "Aristocats" were permitted entry. He liked to have them around when he took his morning siesta. They helped him sleep. There were three of them now: Charo, Michu and Sasha, all long-haired, pedigreed, perfectly groomed Persians...beautiful creatures...only the best. The servants fed them fresh calves' liver, hamburger meat and choice pieces of fish, bought at New York's finest stores and then tastefully prepared by Uda-San.

John had always been attached to his cats. He loved their curious little sounds, their comforting purring, the softness of their fur, their seeming ability to communicate telepathically, their mystical significance, their mythical resonance.

Two years ago, in the spring, he'd lost two of them. A baby Russian Blue got sick and had to be put to sleep. John held the animal in his arms as the vet gave it the injection, and later he cried. Then, his favorite cat, Alice, fell from an open window, and again he wept. Too much death. Too much sadness.

DREAM POWER

IN EARLY 1978, A FEW MONTHS AFTER SEAN'S SECOND birthday, John was beginning to grow weary of spending all day in his bedroom, floating through the afternoons, stroking the cats, sleeping and smoking and reading and jotting the occasional note, perhaps something to use at a future date, in a song or maybe another novel. Often, Sean was off in Central Park with Helen, and Yoko was having her cards read by the O. And John, stoned on Thai, would watch TV, bemused by advertisements for the Broadway show *Beatlemania*.

They don't need me anymore. The clones do it better!

He knew, if he was going to spend three more years essentially in seclusion in the Dakota, he was going to have to find a better way to fill the time. So he filled the time by teaching himself to program dreams. *Dream Power*, he called it, after a book of the same name. John was quickly able to master the technique, and it became his primary means of escape.

Dream Power is self-hypnosis. John lay in bed, totally relaxed, stoned on Thai, hovering on the edge of sleep. He concentrated on whatever he wanted to dream about. If it was sex, he'd fix in his mind's eye an image of the woman he wanted to make love to. Then he'd count backwards from ten. Before reaching one, he'd be asleep, the image set in his mind carried over to the dream.

Once asleep, though, he lost control of the dream, and the plot would take bizarre twists. The second and third dream in each sequence never had any relation to the original programmed dream. Often he'd find himself back in England, twenty years earlier. He'd dream of Liverpool or Paul. Or he'd have a sex dream about George Harrison, which would startle and confuse him. He was furious at George since the publication of his autobiography, *I Me Mine*, which mentioned Lennon only in passing. *What the fuck is this? I did more for fucking George than anybody. Who did he bloody come to when he was having trouble finishing a song? Bloody hell! The bloody bastard doesn't exist anymore as far as I'm concerned!*

But what could have possibly inspired such a dream, he wondered. Was it a visit to the doctor for a prostate examination? It was a unique experience having a doctor's finger probing his asshole. But still, why would that make him dream about George? He didn't know.

John enjoyed dreaming so much that he spent as much time as possible sleeping. Using Dream Power to program one sex dream after another, he'd spend the afternoon in effect making love to Yoko or May Pang, the young Chinese woman who started out as his personal secretary in 1970 but soon became his mistress.

Then he started feeling guilty about sleeping 16 hours a day—or longer. He needed to do something more constructive. Yoko suggested he record all his dreams in detail in a dream diary. Not only would this be an excellent creative exercise, John thought, but the dreams would give him insight into his relationship with Yoko.

The symbols in dreams had always fascinated him. What did they reveal? What was their relationship to reality? Immediately upon waking, he'd write down everything he could remember.

There was so little happening in John's life for the first five months of 1978, he'd virtually forsaken reality for dreams. It was a season of dreams, and most of them were about having sex with celebrities. Sometimes he tried to interpret them and look for patterns. Perhaps, he thought, he could psychoanalyze himself and achieve a cure. Perhaps dreaming would succeed where primal screaming and maharishis had failed.

Though the dreams did not cure him, they did give Yoko the opportunity to understand John better. She read his dream journals daily and always knew exactly what was on his mind.

One afternoon John dreamed he was in bed trying to make love to a dark-haired, Asian movie star: They're both fully dressed. John is kissing her on the lips. But every time he tries to slip his hand up her skirt and between her legs, she pushes it away. "No," she says. "You can't do that." The more she resists, the more excited John gets. They're in a small room of an old country house. At the foot of the bed, a fire blazes in a stone fireplace. Everything in the room is old: the big oak dresser, the hairbrushes and jewelry and knick-knacks on top, the small jade Buddha, who appears to be watching, right in the center. On the wall are a portrait of a stern-looking ancestor in a white bonnet; a framed list of the children's daily chores and activities, such as "9 A.M.—lessons"; and antique farm implements, a pitchfork and plow harness mounted like art objects. He looks out the window. There's a manmade pond, like at his estate in Ascot, but it's frozen over. Beyond the pond there are woods, and playing at the edge of the woods, white-tailed deer. Then he takes the movie star's hand and, like superheros, they fly out the window and, high above the earth, look down at the house.

Another afternoon John dreamed he was with Elvis Presley at a party in the Dakota kitchen: The kitchen table is piled high with hors d'oeuvres. The room is mobbed, everybody grabbing food from the table. Lennon and Presley are the only celebrities there. John doesn't know anybody; he feels out of place in his own house. Nobody's paying attention to him. Everybody has gathered around Elvis. John, drinking a cup of black coffee, tries to get close to Elvis so he can talk to him, but the people won't let him near. "Elvis!" John shouts across the room, but Presley doesn't seem to hear him. Then Elvis approaches John and motions with his head to follow him. They're in John's bedroom. Elvis is sitting on John's bed. John is fiddling with the TV.

In another dream, John and a pregnant Yoko are riding in a limousine through a working-class area of London. The twisting streets are mobbed with people selling used clothing; old women hang out the windows of decaying buildings, shouting things. Other people come running up to the car and pound on the windows. John and Yoko are frightened; they hug each other tightly. Then, hand-in-hand, they're walking up a staircase in an industrial building. They're in a photographer's studio. A photographer wearing a red and black striped sweater is taking photos of a nude woman posing against a graffiti-covered wall.

John often dreamed of transformation. Chairs turn into people. Trees turn into clocks. People turn into animals. In one transformation dream, John is sitting in a hotel room in Los Angeles, staring out the window at an old man walking on Sunset Boulevard. Then John is on the street, naked, facing the old man, smelling his foul breath, staring at his toothless mouth. John's terrified. He doesn't understand what he's doing outside. He doesn't want to be there. The man turns into a wolf.

Later, analyzing the dream, John decided that the wolf was a symbol of his anger.

AFTERNOON

By 1980, John had lost all desire to record his dreams in detail. Naturally, this racked him with guilt, especially when Yoko chided him for his lethargy. "It's important!" she'd tell him. Time and again John would sheepishly agree with her that he must keep a dream journal. But he couldn't find the energy. *Dream of M*, was about the best he could do when he awoke from his after-breakfast siesta around noon. Then he'd sit in bed thinking about how to fill the hours of yet another empty day.

He was certainly in no mood to hang around with people, except maybe Yoko. It would be nice, he thought, just to sit with her, smoke cigarettes and talk. But Yoko was always busy downstairs, making money, plotting the future. Sean was always off someplace with his nanny. Besides, Sean had been acting up lately, and John didn't particularly enjoy being a daddy when Sean was out of control.

Lighting another Gitane, John gazed out the window at Central Park. He studied the sky and each day diligently noted the weather conditions. No matter how lethargic he felt, he always found the energy to contemplate the weather. It was a quasi-religious ritual. The weather, he thought, was important. He was skilled at representing atmospheric conditions symbolically. Like a TV weatherman, he developed graphics for sunny days, partly sunny days, cloudy days and rainy days. His suns had intricately drawn faces that not only gave subtle indications of their intensity, but also showed what effect the weather was having on his mood. He drew angry suns roasting the earth; benevolent suns, beaming peacefully, eyes closed with satisfaction; and laughing suns mocking him in the sky. By the end of the year he'd created an animated flip-page book of 365 days of ever-changing weather conditions. His weather symbols set the tone for each day.

Then he reflected upon the events of the day, rating it with a sign he drew next to the weather symbol. These signs were picture frames, with strings holding them on the wall. The sign itself was rectangular. The string was a triangle on top of the rectangle. The nail was a dot at the apex of the triangle. Inside the rectangle were ordinary words that rated the quality of the day, whether it was good, bad, or in between, with occasional variations to denote unusual traumas or ecstasies.

John had no illusions in 1980 about what his life had become. One good day per week was the most he dared to hope for. Life, for the most part, had gotten tough, just like the TV commercial for Ban Roll-On deodorant said.

Though he loved watching TV, reading, he felt, was a far more constructive way to kill the afternoon. A voracious, eclectic reader, he soaked up everything, stopping only when his eyes grew tired. He read extensively on philosophy, religion, the occult, psychology, history, science, nutrition and self-improvement.

Obsessed with the idea of improving his vision, John read books that explained how to achieve perfect sight through eye exercise. He'd always hated wearing glasses. As a teenager he'd considered them "sissy," a sign of weakness. He'd rather be half-blind than have to wear the damn things, even at the movies. Now he thought they were simply a crutch, that if he only had the willpower, he'd be able to throw them away.

John did the prescribed exercises in brief spurts. But again, he couldn't find the discipline to exercise daily for at least six months, which his books said was the only way to attain the desired results. In his frustration he chastised himself. Yet, even without the exercises there had been brief moments when he did experience perfect vision without glasses. Unfortunately, such a moment had not come in a long time. Once it had happened right after making love with Yoko. All his tension had vanished in a magnificent orgasm. He was totally relaxed and for an instant he had the eyesight of an eagle.

Though nonfiction and self-improvement were his staples, John occasionally read a novel. Henry Miller's *Black Spring*, a raunchy, nostalgic memoir of his days in 1930's Paris, was one book Lennon enjoyed enormously. But it also made him sad because it reminded him of that crazed time in his own life, playing strip joints in Hamburg, Germany, with Stuart Sutcliffe and the other Beatles.

Bearing a strong resemblance to James Dean, Stu was John's closest friend and his roommate at the Liverpool College of Art. John admired his intellect and artistic ability—he was a gifted painter. When Stu won prize money in an art contest, John encouraged him to buy a bass guitar and join the Beatles, which he did, in 1959, though he could barely play and had little talent for music.

After a concert at Litherland Town Hall, in one of Liverpool's rougher neighborhoods, the band was ambushed by a gang of thugs. Stu, the smallest and frailest of the group, was repeatedly kicked in the head by one of the gang members, who was wearing steel-tipped hobnail boots. It was an injury from which Sutcliffe never recovered.

Traveling with the band to Hamburg in 1960, Stu met Astrid Kirchherr, a photographer. They fell in love. Astrid was the first person to photograph the Beatles "artistically," and she was instrumental in helping them find their sartorial style—cutting their hair, designing their clothes.

Stu left the Beatles, remaining behind in Hamburg with Astrid. The last year of his life was plagued by agonizing headaches. Between headaches, he painted frantically, in fantastically bright colors. He died of a brain hemorrhage at 21. The memories would haunt John for the rest of his life.

Hunter S. Thompson's *Fear and Loathing in Las Vegas* was another book that blew John's mind. He was so taken by it, he imagined himself playing Thompson in the movie.

Thompson wrote: "The radio was screaming: 'Power to the people right on!' John Lennon's political song ten years too late. 'That poor fool should have stayed where he was,' said my attorney. 'Punks like that just get in the way when they try to be serious.'"

In his story *The Ballad of John and Yoko*, Lennon admitted: "I wrote and recorded the rather embarrassing *Power to the People* ten years too late (as the now-famous Hunter 'Fear and Loathing for a Living' Thompson pointed out in his Vegas book)."

Skywriting by Word of Mouth contains two more Thompson references: "Fear and Loathing at the Vatican" and "Fear and Loathing Wherever I Can Find It."

Helter Skelter, the Vincent Bugliosi book about the Manson murders, was yet another story that gave Lennon something to think about. It was the height of madness that a song Paul wrote for the "White Album" about a slide in an amusement park had inspired Charles Manson to attempt to start a race war by committing mass murder. The book scared the shit out of Lennon.

John's favorite reading materials were newspapers and, to a lesser degree, magazines. He read the three New York dailies—the *Times,* the *News* and the *Post*—regularly, keeping an eye open for fabrications about his life. He also subscribed to a clipping service that kept him supplied with any Lennon/Ono article that appeared in any major English-language periodical.

John was fascinated by an artist, Alexa Grace, whom he referred to as "A." John had met her in Martha's Vineyard during a 1975 sailing expedition. He considered having an affair with her but was convinced that doing so would break up his marriage. Grace's illustrations occasionally appeared in *The New York Times,* and John was so enchanted by them that he always made a point of clipping them.

John saved everything that caught his fancy, such as Calvin Klein ads with pictures of Brooke Shields and postcards from Liverpool with pictures of Mendips and Strawberry Fields. He used some of this material to decorate the covers of his diaries. Pasted on the 1977 cover was a picture of an ancient Egyptian statue; on the 1978 cover was a Japanese-style graphic of reeds and flowers; on the 1979 cover was a drawing of John wearing headphones set against the backdrop of a futuristic city. "Listen to this picture," read the caption.

As he documented his world with his own writings and drawings, the print media provided parallel commentary, not only on incidents that affected him directly, but on cosmic events that he found meaningful. Deeply impressed by an article that appeared in *The New York Times* explaining how scientists had arrived at a more accurate estimate of the age of the universe, John clipped it and filed it.

He also saved a bit of prose that he found touching—the last few lines of a "fictional memoir" by Ken Kesey, from the October 1979 issue of *Esquire* magazine, titled "The Day After Superman Died." It was about the death of Neal Cassady, friend and muse to writer Jack Kerouac. It read:

Young Cassius Clay.

Young Mailer.

Young Miller.

Young Jack Kerouac before you fractured your football career at Columbia and popped your hernia in Esquire. Young Sandy without your credit card bare. Young Devlin. Young Dylan. Young Lennon. Young lovers wherever you are. Come back and remember and go away and come back.

Attendance mandatory but not required.

In mid-September 1979, stories began appearing in the press saying that Paul, George and Ringo—the 3 B's—had agreed to perform a series of benefit concerts to save the Vietnamese and Cambodian Boat People. A Beatles reunion, it was estimated, would raise $300 million dollars. But John had refused to have anything to do with it, particularly after UN Secretary General Kurt Waldheim—a former Nazi—personally asked him to perform.

In the September 25, 1979, edition of *The New York Post,* which coincidentally was hyping an upcoming piece on the "secrets of the celebrities, eccentrics and ghosts who call the Dakota home," an editorial titled "Nowhere Man" appeared. It read:

For the tragic Boat people of Vietnam and Cambodia who have had to run for their lives and face an uncertain future in the inhospitable refugee camps of Southeast Asia, it is always a hard day's night eight days a week.

Not for them the ticket to ride on a yellow submarine. All they may need is love, but the proposed Beatles concert...is being jeopardized by John Lennon, who has probably written more of compassion and the need to help the less fortunate than any other lyricist.

Lennon is now the resident recluse of the Dakota, one of New York's most luxurious apartment buildings where, among other diversions, he and his wife Yoko Ono own five apartments. Lennon has done well out of his songs of love, but is in danger of becoming, in his own words, a "Nowhere Man."

Is he now saying that we have been his fools on the hill, that even the plight of the Boat People cannot now buy his love?

Surely, with a little help from his friends, we can work it out.... In a recent public letter to the millions who have bought Lennon's songs and enriched him, Lennon and Yoko Ono claimed that what they had tried to achieve in the past they now sought by wishing, that their silence was the silence "of love and not indifference."

Wishing and praying will not help the Boat People. Lennon should listen to the words of one of his own most famous songs:

There's nothing you can do that can't be done...

All you need, John Lennon, is love.

Once it would have driven him into a primal rage. Now he simply filed it without comment.

The supermarket tabloids were John's favorite newspapers and the gossip they provided was an endless source of amusement. He read every issue of *The National Enquirer*, *The Midnight Globe*, and *The National Star* as they came off the press.

The majority of clippings that he saved were from these tabloids. A story from a 1979 issue of the *Enquirer*, "The Beatles Ten Years Later," especially caught his attention. John was astonished by the accuracy of the stuff the *Enquirer* dug up on the Beatles. He could never figure out how they got their information. Gossip-wise, he thought the tabloids were far more accurate than the so-called straight press. The respectable papers always got everything wrong, and they refused to run stories that the tabloids played up in a big way.

John assumed that if the dirt the *Enquirer* dug up on the Beatles was accurate, then most of the other stuff the tabloids printed at least had a nodding acquaintance with the truth, particularly the UFO stories. UFO stories were the other reason he loved the tabloids. He not only believed in UFOs, he was obsessed by them. In *Nobody Told Me*, which he recorded during the *Double Fantasy* sessions (it would later appear on *Milk and Honey*), he sang about UFOs over New York. On the night of August 23, 1974, while standing naked on the terrace of May Pang's East 52nd Street apartment, he had seen a UFO hovering over the East River. It was only a matter of time before the aliens made contact, he believed, and he could hardly wait. Maybe, he thought, they'd take him with them.

Few things gave Yoko more pleasure than feeding a story to one of the local New York papers and then have it appear word-for-word as she dictated it. A certain *Daily News* reporter was always happy to oblige. He'd print anything she told him. Once, though, there was a serious misunderstanding. The *News* reported that Yoko worked for the CIA. She was furious; she couldn't understand how the reporter could suggest such a ridiculous thing. But John thought it was hilarious, which upset Yoko even more.

"It was a joke, Mother," he said, trying to calm her down. "You can't take these things seriously."

In 1977, John was preparing for a five-month-long visit to Japan and Hong Kong, the first of three such trips he'd make in three consecutive years. He began devoting his afternoons to studying the Japanese language, listening to audio cassettes, taking lessons at the Berlitz school and calligraphically printing the Japanese alphabet. Quietly, he grew proficient at the language and knew more than he let on. Not only did he want to be able to communicate in Japan, but he wanted to understand what Yoko was saying to the Japanese servants and what the servants were saying to each other.

The purpose of the Japan journey was to introduce Sean to Yoko's family. In Japan, John dressed in a black suit and tie to show proper respect when he met the Onos.

He went bicycle riding with Yoko's "Japan-nieces." He took the Japan-nieces on a family picnic. He was a very proud daddy when Sean placed first in an art contest at a street festival. He prayed at Buddhist shrines near Kyoto as Elliot Mintz—who was flown in to keep him company—watched.

He visited a blind shiatsu who diagnosed his chronic problems with constipation and diarrhea by touching his abdomen. The shiatsu told him that he had weak intestines but was otherwise very healthy and would live to a ripe old age.

John was devastated when he learned on August 16 that Elvis Presley had died. He sent flowers to Graceland. He couldn't believe that the man who inspired him to play rock 'n' roll was gone—he was only 42.

Primarily, though, the trip was a gastronomic odyssey through Hong Kong and Tokyo. At first, John ate in a different restaurant every night and kept as a souvenir the restaurant's business card or menu. He critiqued the food, rating each dish and bottle of wine. He was obsessed with finding the perfect Tokyo eatery. A good meal was a joyous event, a bad meal a cause for despair. His standards were high, his opinions harsh. He thought the majority of

Tokyo's restaurants were grease pits, particularly the ones specializing in Chinese food. Though he did manage to locate one commendable Peking duck joint, his adventurous eating resulted mostly in indigestion and diarrhea.

The final two months of his stay in Japan, John confined himself to the Presidential suite of Tokyo's best hotel, the Okura, and ate only room service toast and tea. A highlight of his stay was spotting John Belushi in the lobby. Lennon thought Belushi's portrayal of Jake Blues was hysterical and wanted to tell him so. But he didn't approach the *Saturday Night Live* star, merely stared at him from a respectful distance, not wanting to invade his privacy like a common fan. He then returned to his room and sat in bed with his diary, contemplating his digestive tract.

LENNON'S COMPLAINT

IT WAS 1963 AND THE BEATLES WERE BACKSTAGE AT A concert hall somewhere in northern England, scheduled to go on in fifteen minutes. John couldn't remember exactly where they were; maybe Manchester, maybe Sheffield ...it didn't really matter anymore. Beatlemania was already out of hand; everything was a blur. Sitting in the dressing room with the others, tuning his guitar, John got a sudden urge for an immediate fucking—a knee trembler—and dispatched Neil Aspinall, the road manager, to retrieve the nearest blonde, preferably one with big tits. Moments later Neil returned with the girl. She was a little bit drunk and not a day over 17— exactly what John wanted. He didn't say a word; he just stood her up against the wall, reached under her skirt, ripped off her knickers, whipped out his cock and shoved it in. But when he pulled out, blood was oozing from the head of his prick and everybody was laughing. John was horrified. He'd ruptured a membrane in his foreskin.

"You fuckin' cow!" he screamed at the dumbfounded girl. "What did you do to me fuckin' cock?"

John was going to slap her, but Neil restrained him. "Get out there and play your fuckin' guitar, you bloody bastard," he said, gently guiding him towards the stage; the others were already out there, waiting.

"I'll never fuck again!" John cried, sticking his bleeding cock back in his pants and walking onstage, into the maw of the shrieking crowd.

Things had calmed down considerably in the ensuing 17 years. They'd calmed down so much that by 1980 the new and sensitive John Lennon had been reduced to a wanker, gratifying himself morning, noon, and night, his life passing in a blur of wank...*Call me fucking Portnoy!*

The problem was that Yoko had lost all interest in sex. In the song *No, No, No,* on *Season of Glass,* an album she recorded after John's death, she sang of seeing broken glass when they made love.

This particular marital difficulty began in March 1975, as soon as Yoko realized she was pregnant. Sex with John became erratic, and Lennon began to wonder if his wife had already forgotten the reason he ran away for 18 months with May Pang. Then, after Sean's birth, sex became even less frequent. John began spending his days staring out his bedroom window, overwhelmed by the number of gorgeous women in New York City.

Again, John started slipping away to see May. Once he told Yoko he was going to the hospital to visit Richard Ross, a mutual friend of his and May's who was being treated for leukemia. He met May in the hospital room. Richard volunteered to take a long walk. The last time John and May ever made love was in Richard's hospital bed. After that, John stopped seeing her because he could not deal with the guilt and the fear of being found out.

He still needed sex. With his access to groupies and mistresses cut off, it's likely the masseuses who came to the Dakota every week were also massaging less traditional body parts. What exactly did Ringo see when he visited Lennon at the Dakota one afternoon, arriving in the middle of a "shiatsu" session?

It's also possible that with cheap thrills hard to come by in 1980, the so-called shiatsu was the erotic highlight of Lennon's grim week, and that on the weeks the masseuses canceled, Lennon sank into despair. The massage sessions were his only real pleasure, and a week without a massage was a week of unrelenting pain, relieved only by compulsive wanking.

THE OCCULT ARTS

N 1977, YOKO, WITH JOHN'S BLESSING, SPENT A WEEK IN South America studying magic with Lena, a seven-foot-tall Columbian witch. A business associate who normally specialized in acquiring "magical" antiques introduced Ono to Lena as a special favor. Lena had a reputation for being the most powerful sorceress on the continent. Yoko paid her $60,000 to acquire the power to cast spells. At first John was a little disturbed by how much money Yoko had spent, but he was ultimately delighted with the results. Never revealing the exact details, John was convinced that Mother was now magically cursing business adversaries to get what she wanted.

Yoko was skilled, too, at doing her own astrological and numerological calculations. One of the reasons she and John chose to live at the Dakota was because the address—1 West 72nd Street, Apartment 72—had "good numbers." The numbers provided sympathetic vibrations that enhanced John and Yoko's magical powers.

In 1978, a man who did not identify himself left a message for John and Yoko at the Dakota. He warned them that he had studied the black arts and was now devoting all his energies to controlling the Lennons. John took the threat very seriously but felt confident this sorcerer could do nothing to harm them. Since he and Yoko understood magic, they'd be able to counter any spell cast upon them with a more powerful spell.

The Lennons saw magic as both an instrument of crisis management and the ideal weapon. Because they had in abundance the magician's most important tool—a powerful imagination—they believed that they could use magic to ultimately control the entire universe.

They found magic's poetic irrationality irresistibly appealing. In their widely published 1979 "Love Letter to the People," they proclaimed: "Magic is logical." According to classic texts on the subject, magic is a system based on the belief that within every person lies the Divine spark. Man is a miniature image of God, and the universe is a human organism on a gigantic scale. Impulses like love and hate, which are found within everyone, exist in the universe as well. By focusing his powers of concentration and imagination on a single idea or emotion, a magician has the ability to absorb these universal impulses and bend them to his will.

John and Yoko were forever boiling over with intense emotions. They had learned that these emotions carry a force that will profoundly affect the person at whom they're directed.

The laws of magic dictate that events on earth run parallel to events in the heavens. Both are dependent upon the workings of God. It's possible for a skilled magician to affect the course of events in the sky by manipulating events on earth.

Yoko's office in Studio One is a perfect example of this "As Above, So Below" logic. On the ceiling is painted a blue sky filled with puffy white clouds. This is magical mimicry; Yoko created her own "favorable" sky in a sealed room to protect herself from the real, hostile sky outside. It was the ideal room in which to conduct business. Here, too, were Yoko's 26th Dynasty Egyptian antiques, potent magical talismans acquired during a January 1979 journey to the pyramids outside Cairo. John had accompanied Yoko on this field trip and they had spent a night inside The Great Pyramid, an experience that thrilled and energized the Lennons, heightening their magical powers—or so Yoko said.

The only difficulty, really, was that to truly succeed in magic, the magician had to devote his entire life to it, and neither John nor Yoko was willing to make that kind of commitment. Magic, like clairvoyance achieved through the dedicated practice of yoga, simply demanded too much time and willpower. What the Lennons really needed was an easier way to achieve the results that magic promised. To control the entire universe wasn't really necessary. If they could only peer into the future occasionally, then they could prepare themselves for any nasty tricks the universe might hold in store. That's what the professional psychics were for. And they would remain on the payroll until John developed a consistently clear vision of the future, which Yoko believed was a stong possibility. She just wished he'd hurry up and do it.

THE BOOK OF NUMBERS

LONG BEFORE DISCOVERING NUMEROLOGY, JOHN HAD been aware of the strong presence of the number 9 in his life. He and Sean were both born on October 9. There are Beatles songs titled *One After 909* and *Revolution 9*. The cover of Lennon's *Walls and Bridges* album, which contains the song *No. 9 Dream,* is a drawing he did in school when he was 11 years old. It's a picture of a soccer game, and prominently displayed on the jersey of one of the players is number 9. Brian Epstein first saw the Beatles at The Cavern on November 9, 1961. Exactly five years later on November 9, John met Yoko. The Beatles' first recording contract, with EMI, was signed on May 9, 1962. His mother, Julia, lived at 9 Newcastle Road. John had always written off these facts as mere coincidence, though he did consider 9 his lucky number—even after learning from Yoko that 9, pronounced *ku* in Japanese, is a homonym of the word for pain and suffering.

During his years of seclusion, Lennon dove headlong into numerology. It was just what he needed. Numerology could quickly be applied to any situation to get a preliminary reading on the future.

Simple, compelling, and poetic, the arcane laws of numerology have the power to make even the staunchest skeptic *want* to believe in it. Like playing the lottery, it can be addictive. After learning about numerology, John and Yoko were unable to walk out of the house without finding mystical significance in every license plate, address, and street sign. They would not so much as dial a telephone number without first consulting their bible, *Cheiro's Book of Numbers,* which could have been subtitled *Numerology Made Easy.*

According to Cheiro—who had impressed both Mark Twain and Oscar Wilde with his occult powers—all numbers have a distinct vibration. The numbers 1 to 9 make a complete set of vibrations. The most important number in anybody's life is the day of the month on which he or she was born. At that moment the universe's overall rate of vibration is indelibly stamped on a person's character and destiny. Since John was born on October 9, he was a number 9.

The number of your name, according to Cheiro, is the second most important number. Though other numerologists consider your name number more important than your birth number, John and Yoko were inclined to agree with Cheiro. But all numerologists are in agreement that your name and birth number have to be considered simultaneously. Nobody, they say, is named by accident. Your name is preordained by the universe; it contains your essence, and like your birth number, reveals your character and destiny. By changing your name you can change your character and destiny. Your birth number, of course, can never be changed.

Name numbers are based on the Hebrew alphabet. Each letter is given a numerical value from 1 to 8 as follows:
A=1 B=2 C=3 D=4 E=5 F=8 G=3 H=5 I=1 J=1 K=2 L=3 M=4 N=5 O=7 P=8 Q=1 R=2 S=3 T=4 U=6 V=6 W=6 X=5 Y=1 Z=7

Though something is lost when translated into the Roman alphabet, numerologists choose to ignore this inconvenient detail.

When calculating a name or birth number, all two-digit numbers (though they have their own significance, which must be taken into consideration) are added together to form a single-digit number. Therefore, 9, 18 and 27 are all number 9's. Upon reading Cheiro, John realized that the three most important people in his life—Sean, born October 9; Yoko, born February 18; and Paul McCartney, born June 18—were 9's. The fact that they shared his birth number was enough to make John believe in numerology.

Here is a condensed version of what Cheiro wrote: *Number 9 persons are fighters in all they attempt in life. They usually have difficult times in their early years but generally are in the end successful by their grit, strong will and determination. They are hasty in temper, impulsive, independent and desire to be their own masters.*

When number 9 is noticed to be more than usually dominant in the dates and events of their lives, they will be found to make great enemies, to cause strife and opposition wherever they may be and are often wounded or killed either in warfare or in the battle of life.

They have great courage and make excellent leaders in any cause they espouse.

Their greatest dangers arise from foolhardiness and impulsiveness in word and actions.

They generally have quarrels and strife in their home life.

They strongly resent criticism. They like to be "looked up to" and recognized as "head of the house." For affection and sympathy they will do almost anything, and men of this number can be made the greatest fools of if some woman gets to pulling at their heart strings.

This number 9 is the only number that when multiplied by any number always reproduces itself. The number 9 represents the Planet Mars, which in astrology is the ruler of the zodiacal sign Aries, which is the sign of the Zodiac that governs England. The number 9 is an emblem of matter that can never be destroyed. At the 9th hour the savior died on the cross. All ancient races encouraged a fear of the number 9. The number 9 is considered a fortunate number to be born under, provided the man or woman does not ask for a peaceful or monotonous life and can control their nature by not making enemies.

Impressed by Cheiro's analysis, John felt as if the book was speaking directly to him.

He read of the occult symbolism of Yoko and Paul's birth number, 18. By the time he finished, he was certain that he'd discovered a book of truth. But the truth was disturbing. Just as number 9 appeared to be a perfect description of himself, 18 was an equally insightful depiction of his two main creative partners.

The symbol for number 18, Cheiro wrote, is *a rayed moon from which drops of blood are falling; a wolf and hungry dog are seen below catching the falling drops of blood in their open mouths, while still lower, a crab is hastening to join them. It is symbolic of materialism striving to destroy the spiritual side of the nature. It generally associates a person with bitter quarrels, even family ones, war, social upheavals, revolutions; and in some cases it indicates making money and position through wars. It is a warning of treachery, deception by others, also danger from explosions. When this "compound" number appears in working out dates in advance, such a date should be taken with a great amount of care, caution and circumspection.*

Using Cheiro's alphabet chart, John calculated the numerical value of his own name. He understood that for a true reading he'd have to be thorough and figure out the numbers for his myriad names and nicknames.

JOHN	WINSTON	LENNON
1755	6153475	355575
18=9	31=4	30=3
9 +	4 +	3 = 16=7

JOHN	ONO	LENNON
	757	
	19=10=1	
9 +	1 +	3 = 13=4

JOHN	WINSTON	ONO	LENNON
9 +	4 +	1 +	3 = 17=8

JOHNNY	WALRUS	DR	WINSTON	O'BOOGIE
175551	613263	42		7 277315
24=6	21=3	6		32=5
		6 +	4 +	5 = 15=6

JOHN	LENNON
9 +	3 = 12=3

There was much to consider. The patterns had to be carefully interpreted. The numbers had to be matched against the period of his life when each particular name was being used.

Born John Winston Lennon, he legally changed his name to John Ono Lennon one month after marrying Yoko. His green card read John *Winston* Ono Lennon, but now he only used the name Winston facetiously, as in Dr. Winston O'Boogie, the alter ego under which he subscribed to magazines. Twenty years ago, in Liverpool, everybody called him Johnny, and even today a few people still called him that. Of course, the self-imposed nickname "Walrus" must not be overlooked.

The one fact that stood out like a searchlight was that "John" alone equaled 18, or 9—the two most significant numbers in his life. His first name vibrated sympathetically with his birth number, Sean's birth number, and Yoko's birth number. This meant that his life was in harmony. But 16, the compound number of the name on his birth certificate, was troubling. Known as The Shattered Citadel, its symbol is a *tower struck by lightning from which a man is falling with a crown on his head. It gives warning of some strange fatality awaiting one.* Reduced to 7, though, the results were happier.

Sevens, said Cheiro, *make extremely good writers, painters or poets, but in everything they do, they sooner or later show a peculiar philosophical outlook on life that tinges all their work. They often become rich by their original ideas or methods of business but they are just as likely to make large donations to charity. They create a religion of their own, but one that appeals to the imagination and is based on the mysterious. They have wonderful dreams and a great leaning to occultism; they have a gift of intuition, clairvoyance, and a peculiar quieting magnetism of their own that has a great influence on others.*

Now that's more like it, John thought. But only his aunt and mother had ever called him John Winston Lennon, at least out loud. People called him John—number 9 pure and simple! "John Lennon" was 12 or 3. "Lennon" alone was also 3. Three and 12 vibrated sympathetically with 9. Twelve, John had to admit, was also accurate in many ways. The number of *suffering and anxiety of the mind, it is indicated as "the sacrifice" or "the victim" and generally foreshadows one being sacrificed for the plans or intrigues of others.* Threes, on the other hand, love discipline and *rise to the highest positions in any profession they choose.* "Walrus," too, was a 3.

He then considered his current full name, John Ono Lennon, and was thoroughly discouraged. If he had changed his destiny by changing his name, the change was from bad to worse. Thirteen is the number of death, upheaval and destruction. *It's a symbol of power which if wrongly used will wreak destruction upon itself.* Though all single-digit numbers in Cheiro are positive in some way, 4 is the least positive. People with this number *make a great number of secret enemies who constantly work against them...and they instinctively rebel against rules and regulations. They often rebel against constitutional authority and set up new rules and regulations either in domestic or public life. They are positive and unconventional in their views and opinions. They are highly strung and sensitive, very easily wounded in their feelings, inclined to feel lonely and isolated in the world and are likely to become despondent and melancholy.*

But all his nicknames equalled 3 or 6, and that was good. Six, symbolic of the planet Venus, was the number of love. *All number 6 people are extremely magnetic; they attract others to them and are loved and often worshipped by those under them.*

No question about it, there was a lot of good in the numbers.

The problem was that the bad seemed to overwhelm it; the numbers were stacked against him. There were too many indications of catastrophe, violence, premature death. But John didn't need the *Book of Numbers* to tell him that. He had felt it in his soul for as long as he could remember. Psychics could sense it when they looked at him. The numbers only confirmed it.

He then calculated the names of his wife and sons.

YOKO	ONO	YOKO	ONO	LENNON	
1727	757	8 +	1 +	3 = 12=3	
17=8	19=10=1				
8 +	1 = 9!!!				

SEAN	ONO	LENNON	
3515			
14=5			
5 +	1 +	3 = 9!!!	

SEAN	TARO	ONO	LENNON	
	4127			
	14=5			
5 +	5 +	1 +	3 = 14=5	

JOHN	CHARLES	JULIAN		LENNON
	3512353	163115		
	22=4	17=8		
9 +	4 +	8 +		3 = 24=6

To John's delight and astonishment, Sean and Yoko were both 9's! And Yoko Ono Lennon, the name on their marriage certificate, was exactly the same as John Lennon (and Walrus)—12 and 3! The names and birth numbers of his entire family were harmonious in every imaginable configuration! There was nothing more that needed to be considered here. John was glad that both Sean and his middle name, Taro, were 5's, and his entire name, Sean Taro Ono Lennon, was also 5. Fives, Cheiro said, *rebound quickly from the heaviest blows, are quick in thought and have a keen sense of making money.* These were the exact qualities Sean would need to survive.

Julian's name, too, was full of good Lennon vibrations. But most people didn't know his name was John Charles Julian (John sometimes called him JCJ), named after his father, his mother's father and his father's mother, Julia. Everybody called him Julian Lennon, and that was 8+3=11=2.

George Harrison waves a Union Jack as the Beatles arrive at London Airport, February 1964. Though John rarely saw any of the "three B's" in his final years, they were often in his thoughts and dreams.

Eleven, which *gives warnings of hidden dangers, trials, and treachery from others* summed it up for his first son. Two, also, was not a good number. Though *imaginative, artistic, romantic, and inventive, they are not forceful in carrying out their ideas, nor are they physically strong.* Poor Julian, thought John. His birthday, too, was April 4, the number of secret enemies, easily wounded feelings, loneliness and isolation—the number of John Ono Lennon.

He continued his analysis.

```
BEATLES
2514353
23=5

JAMES        PAUL        MCCARTNEY
11453        8163        433124551
14=5         18=9        28=10=1
5  +         9  +        1  =  15=6

GEORGE       HARRISON—Born February 25=7
357235       51221375
25=7         26=8
7  +         8  =  15=6
```

RICHARD STARKEY
2135124 3412251
18=9   18=9
9 +   9 = 18=9

RINGO   STARR—Born July 7
21537   34122
18=9   12=3
9 +   3 = 12=3

BRIAN   EPSTEIN
22115   5834515
11=2   31=4
2 +   4 = 6

GEORGE MARTIN
357235 412415
25=7   17=8
7 +   8 = 15=6

The deeper John probed, the more he believed. The numerical patterns couldn't be ignored. Nines and 6's were everywhere among the key people of his professional life. No wonder The Beatles were so successful! James Paul McCartney equals George Harrison equals Brian Epstein equals George Martin, equals Johnny! John equals Paul equals Ringo! Ringo Starr equals John Lennon in both single-digit and compound numbers. And George and Ringo have the same birth number. Paul, Dr. Winston O'Boogie, George Harrison and George Martin all have number 15, *a number of occult significance, magic and mystery. The persons represented by it will use every act of magic they can to carry out their purpose.* It must have worked.

The connections were mind-boggling. Twenty-three, the number of The Beatles, symbolized *The Royal Star of the Lion and promised success, help from superiors, and protection from those in high places.* Reduced to 5, Beatles=Sean Taro Ono Lennon. And why not?

CYNTHIA POWELL   LENNON
3154511 876533
20=2   32=5
2 +   5 +   3
                  3 = 10=1

MAY   PANG
411   8153
6   17=8
6 +   8 = 14=5

Not surprisingly to John, Cynthia Lennon alone is 2+3=5, which equals May Pang. Former wife equals former mistress! Cynthia Powell, her maiden name, equals John Winston Lennon, the name he used when he was married to her. Did it not make perfect sense?

```
JULIA      LENNON
16311
12=3  +     3  =  6

FREDDY     LENNON
825441
24=6  +     3  =  9

ALFRED     LENNON
138254
23=5  +     3  =  8

ALF        LENNON
138
12=3  +     3  =  6

MIMI       SMITH
4141       34145
10=1       17=8
1   +      8  =  9

LIVERPOOL
316528773
42=6

PENNY      LANE
85551      3155
24=6       14=5
6   +       5  =  11=2

STRAWBERRY          FIELDS
3421625221          815343
28=10=1             24=6
1   +               6  =  7

CAVERN
316525
22=4
```

So his daddy, Alfred, at least in the more commonly used form of "Freddy," was a 9, too, as was his Aunt Mimi, who raised him! But his daddy and his mother were also 6's—6's among many 6's, including Liverpool itself. Strawberry Fields, which was around the corner from Mendips, the house where he grew up, equals John Winston Lennon. *Poetic!* Penny Lane equals Julian Lennon. Julian's pediatrician, Doctor Basil, who John suspected was the son of his own pediatrician, had his office on Penny Lane. Cavern equals John Ono Lennon, both number 4.

Then John noticed that 1980=18. *The year is a 9!*

DAKOTA (Built 1881=18=9!!!)   1 West 72nd Street Apt 72
412741   9   9
19=10=1

NEW   YORK   CITY
556   1722   3141
16=7   12=3   9
7 +   3   +   9 = 19=10=1

And the last four digits of his phone number:
4437=18=9!

Nines everywhere, even in the year the Dakota was built! There was no end to it. Yoko, when she arranged for the phone number, had seen to it that at least part of it vibrated sympathetically. And the Dakota itself vibrated sympathetically with New York City.

But what did it all mean? Beyond *Watch out for number 9 in all its configurations,* John didn't have a clue.

THE CARDS
ACCORDING
TO SWAN

THE ONLY MAN WITH THE INSIGHT TO HELP JOHN unravel the web of numbers was his full-time psychic and tarot card reader, Charlie Swan. (Only John and Yoko called him Charlie Swan. His real name was John Green.) Lennon trusted and depended upon the bearded, six-foot-six-inch, 250-pound Oracle ("the O") for two good reasons. Not only did he have a genuine psychic gift, but, more important, no matter how bad things looked, Swan never said anything to frighten John. Even during tarot readings, when the death card itself came up under the most inauspicious circumstances, the O was always able to convince Lennon that it meant rebirth or change, not imminent death. Still, John sensed from the look in the O's eyes that something ominous was hanging over him like a black cloud. John couldn't hide his dark vibrations, and it didn't take a psychic to feel them.

Along with tarot, Swan was well versed in astrology and magic—and he was clairvoyant. That's why the Lennons paid him $25,000 per year and set him up rent-free in an enormous loft on Broome Street in Soho.

Yoko had met Swan in 1974, when John was in L.A. with May Pang. When John came home, Yoko introduced him to her new psychic. At the time, Lennon was having nightmarish legal and business problems. His Beatle royalties were frozen at Apple; there was little cash flow. People were suing him left and right. And EMI/Capitol was demanding new material—more "Capitol punishment."

Swan's tarot readings and level-headed financial advice impressed John enormously. By the end of the year, most of the problems seemed to have magically resolved themselves. The

Beatles partnership was formally dissolved; money flowed again. The lawsuits vanished at least temporarily. And by 1976 his contract with EMI/Capitol had expired.

John and Yoko gave Swan a good deal of the credit. With his tarot deck acting as a mystical compass, he'd help them navigate treacherous waters. Swan was now part of the inner circle, their most trusted advisor. They sought his opinions on everything from sex to gold futures. To make him more worldly and clear his karmic circuits, they sent him around the globe by jet, in a westerly direction, in two and one-half days.

Over the years, Swan would earn every penny of his salary. Yoko met with him or spoke to him seven days a week, for hours at a time, constantly calling him in the middle of the night. He did thousands of tarot readings. Sometimes Yoko ventured downtown to meet Swan, but when problems became overwhelming, she wouldn't leave the Dakota. Swan would then be summoned uptown for a meeting under the favorable blue skies of Studio One

And what better way to liven up a dull afternoon than to invite the Oracle to the Dakota and have him peer into the future or take a reading on the present with his magical deck of cards?

The Magician, Swan said, was the card that most closely represented John, and John wholeheartedly agreed. He *was* The Magician, and he pasted the card on the cover of his 1976 journal, after first replacing the face on it with his own face, cut from a photo.

The Magician is the card of creative power. He's a man who is creative both in his art and his home life. He receives his power from above, through a magic wand he holds high over his head. Also above his head is the symbol of eternal life, a horizontal figure 8. Though he can be weak-willed and may use his creative powers for destructive ends, such as getting even with an enemy, The Magician, more than anything, represents the personal will in union with the divine will—a perfect description of John's overriding ambition to merge with God.

Another symbol of eternity, a snake devouring its own tail, encircles The Magician's waist. The snake is also a symbol of The Magician's overpowering sex drive, which if thwarted turns to self-love. The Magician is potentially a compulsive masturbator.

Yoko, according to Swan, was The High Priestess, the card of hidden influence and a symbol of a woman who can potentially destroy her man through selfishness. Symbolic, too, of the Virgin Mary, Mother of Jesus, she holds in her lap the Torah, the scroll of divine law. The High Priestess is a ruthless mystery woman who never divulges her secrets. Strongly intuitive and spiritually enlightened, she's the "keeper of the mysteries of the universe." Her crown is a full moon, suggesting number 18, Yoko's birth number and the card of the moon. The Magician and The High Priestess are the ideal couple, Swan assured them.

Swan's position in the Lenono hierarchy was considerably more elevated than that of a servant. John and Yoko were completely dependent upon him, and he knew it. Though they believed that Swan could see into the future with a high degree of accuracy, clairvoyant powers were not what kept him on the payroll. His greatest talents were insight and common sense. Swan had John and Yoko pegged. Usually Yoko came to him on the verge of hysteria with her daily "emergency." She wasn't interested in hearing the truth. She needed to be calmed down, reassured. Swan was more of a marriage counselor and psychiatrist than a psychic. He always knew just what to say, which generally meant telling her exactly what she wanted to hear.

Sometimes John threatened to divorce Yoko, and these threats left her badly shaken. But Swan knew that John would never divorce her, no matter how miserable the marriage became. There were too many complications, too many legal nightmares. Swan knew that John was just venting his frustrations on Yoko by preying on her worst fears and insecurities.

"It's only a phase," Swan would assure her. "Ride it out. Everything will change for the better."

John and Yoko didn't set foot outside the Dakota without first checking with the Oracle. Before they bought a house or an art object, O took a psychic reading. Did it give off evil vibrations? Was it a good investment? O acted as travel agent. He advised them where to go, the date of departure, the date of return. Was it safe to fly? Or was a voyage by sea a better idea? O told them whom to see and whom not to see; whom to do business with and whom not to do business with; whom to hire and whom to fire. Sometimes they disagreed with him, but usually they followed his advice to the letter. If things didn't work out, Swan took the blame.

For five-hundred dollars a week plus the loft—the best deal he'd ever had—Swan was happy to take responsibility. John felt he'd already been saddled with too much responsibility for too many things. He didn't want to be responsible for *anything*. It was no picnic being a multimillionaire ex-Beatle.

Creatively drained and emotionally exhausted, John felt he had to go into seclusion for the five years following Sean's birth. Swan understood that, no matter what he said, there'd be no talking John out of it. So he supported the decision totally. In 1980 John and Yoko made it clear to Swan that they were determined to face the world again.

Swan assured them that 1980 and 1981 were going to be very big years. Patric Walker, in his February 1980 Libra horoscope, agreed. On August 16, Walker predicted, with the sun eclipsed by the moon in Aquarius, "you will reach a plateau where your life can be controlled, regulated, and at last enjoyed to the full."

John and Yoko clung enthusiastically to these tarot and astrological predictions, regardless of how bleak the future appeared. The darker their lives grew, the more they reminded themselves of the astonishing clarity of Swan's vision. But just to make sure, John tested the O by investing in gold futures.

Like a precious metals broker, Lennon diligently plotted the volatile rise and fall of gold prices. To buy or to sell, that was the question, and every day he sat at the kitchen table conferring with the O and his cards. They argued passionately, with John often ignoring Swan's advice and going with his own hunches. Swan was good on trends, predicting general rises and falls. But the psychic had never been able to predict the price of gold exactly, as John had managed to do one day. This convinced Lennon that he was close to achieving genuine precognitive powers. Nevertheless, he usually bought and sold at the wrong times. It cost him a small fortune, and he chastised himself, wondering why he hadn't listened to the Oracle. Such incidents renewed his faith in the O's powers.

John knew the only surefire way to make money in precious metals was to achieve true clairvoyance. So once again he turned to yoga. Every morning, just as in the old days, he assumed the lotus position and meditated. But the more he meditated, the more he began thinking about the path to enlightenment. Suddenly, like Gandhi, he wanted to free himself from desire, from his trivial obsession with gold futures. It was unfulfilled desire that caused him pain. Without desire there would be no pain. And once he merged with God, the wide range of psychic powers he'd develop would include not only clairvoyance, but also telepathy, the ability to fly through the air, and the ability to know of his past lives.

The more John thought about it, the more he believed it was imperative to again make the effort. Everybody was expecting him to emerge from his five years of seclusion with a new record album. But imagine if he were to step forth a full-blown psychic. Not even Paul McCartney could top that!

John wasn't even sure that he really wanted to record an LP. Having long ago achieved all earthly ambitions, he had no enthusiasm for the music business anymore. He needed to ascend to a higher spiritual plane. If he could develop his psychic powers, he'd be able to face life with newfound energies. It would be a true rebirth. And Yoko would be able to fire all the psychics and astrologers—even Swan.

Yoko assured John time and again that he could do anything he set his mind to, and that psychic powers were well within his reach. John agreed, aware that only prolonged meditation could arouse the "kundalani" serpent energy at the base of his spine. The kundalani would then pass through his six centers of consciousness until it reached the seventh, located at the center of his brain. Only then would he be one with God. He'd know everything—past, present and future.

John had tapped the kundalani in flashes. He could reach the fourth level of consciousness, located at the heart, almost at will. There he could see the divine light, though he preferred to call it the Promised Land. He'd also been to the fifth level—located in the throat—though not through meditation. He'd done it by making love to Yoko. There were crystalline moments in the midst of orgasm when he felt free of all ignorance and delusion. All his thoughts were with God. Once he'd gone as high as the sixth level, located in his forehead. He'd achieved a direct vision of God...on a bloody fucking cross. But that required LSD, and the enlightened yogis said that it didn't count—one could not merge with God through drugs; meditation was the only way.

As hard as he tried, John could not find the willpower to meditate every morning for hours at a time. There were no shortcuts.

Clairvoyance, he finally had to admit, was beyond his reach, and it saddened him. He'd never be able to make money with gold futures. He'd never be a psychic yogi.

BEATLE ECONOMICS

WITH A QUARTERLY APPLE BOARD MEETING IMPENDING, it was fortunate that the stars were properly aligned. According to Yoko's *Town & Country* horoscope, January 1980 was the "best month of the year for matters pertaining to long-term security." But nothing could ever be left to chance; psychics and astrologers still had to be consulted, tarot cards read, numbers calculated.

The questions always remained the same. How is Apple going to try and fuck us this time? How can we stop them? Can we fuck them worse than they can fuck us?

John couldn't bear to think about it. He'd already been forced to think about it for too many years. Yoko was now John's official business representative. It was her job to think about fucking Apple, and she was good at it.

Apple Corps, the Beatles' record company, had undergone a complete metamorphosis in the past decade—it was no longer a record company. It hadn't put out a new album in ten years. Apple was now an accounting firm, darkly known to insiders as Apple Corpse. It collected and distributed money. But one thing hadn't changed at all. Apple remained a testament to the fact that life among the Beatles family was an endlessly bitter contract dispute.

Should any illusion have survived that the Beatles, in 1980, still existed as a rock band, a visit to Apple headquarters in London would have instantaneously shattered it. The office suite itself was a morgue, presided over by managing director Neil Aspinall, who was the original Beatles road manager, and a staff of one. An erratic assortment of gold records, hung with little thought or care, still remained on the walls. And the graffiti-covered door of the original Apple building on Savile Row stood in one corner of Aspinall's immaculate white office, looking strangely out of place.

The only living connection with the Beatles ever to be found at Apple were their children. Occasionally Zak Starr or Julian Lennon —eerily reminiscent of his father—drifted in. Aspinall's office was a refuge, a good place to hang out. The kids liked to sit in an egg-shaped chair with built-in stereo speakers, listening to music. Once, a Beatles admirer whom Zak and Julian had run into at Leicester Square had given them a vial of liquid methadone. But they were still young and hadn't learned the correct way to abuse the drug; they weren't even sure they wanted to abuse it. They showed it to Neil, who, assuming the role of concerned adult, crushed it on the white carpet under his heel and advised them to stick to drinking, like good English lads.

But Aspinall's real job was not high-priced guidance counselor; he was an ambassador between the four ex-Beatles and their empires. Should one ex-Beatle desire to communicate with another ex-Beatle, but not want to see the money-grubbing bastard face-to-face, Aspinall was the man to deliver the message. It was a thankless job, even worse than holding together the last vestiges of a dream that should have been over, yet lived on because of the lawyers and accountants who refused to let it die.

That the Beatles had formally ceased to exist as a performing group in 1971 and that the business partnership had been officially dissolved in 1975 were meaningless facts. Nothing had really been resolved; nothing was ever resolved. Beatles money continued to pour in, and it had to be divvied up.

At the beginning of each year, John, Paul, George and Ringo or their business representatives—all the lawyers and accountants and their assistants and sub-assistants—met at a conference table, either in London or in New York City's Plaza Hotel, along with Aspinall. The representatives, administrative gnomes who ran the individual Beatles' affairs out of their home offices, were facetiously called "Apples." And when they were gathered in those conference rooms, it was their job to fight like animals over their fair share of the Apple royalties. It was guerrilla warfare. There were no rules. All contracts were rendered meaningless. Everybody had gotten burned in the past. If they didn't get burned this time, it only meant they'd get burned the next time. There was no love lost among the Beatles family. The only thing that was certain was that you'd only get as much money as you could force the others to give you.

Dealing with Apple had already driven John to the brink of insanity, and if it wasn't for Yoko, who became his official representative in 1977, he'd have long ago plunged into the abyss. It was one thing doing business with people like Sir Lew Grade, the British show biz mogul who controlled Northern Songs, the Beatles music publishing company. John knew he was a greedy bastard and expected him to do everything in his power to get more than his fair share. It was quite another matter when you realized the people you grew up with, under the pernicious influence of their accountants and lawyers, were also going to take you for every penny you had if you let them.

John was sick of fighting for what he felt he'd already won a hundred times over. He looked upon these meetings as the Damocles Sword the Beatles had always held over his head, suspended by a single hair to constantly remind him of the precariousness of his fortune.

But Yoko enjoyed the battle. She thrived on the fact that the money people resented her as a woman, and hated her guts because she was Yoko Ono in particular. They hated her because they had no choice but to deal with her.

One thing was clear in January 1980: Apple thought that the Lennons had too much money. In the past the company had threatened to cut them off completely, and John and Yoko knew they were serious. If Apple could get away with it, they'd do it. If Yoko didn't march into the conference room and forcefully demand the Lennons' fair share, they wouldn't get a penny.

Even Neil Aspinall, John's old public school buddy, was, like everybody else, demanding a bigger piece of the pie. He'd been with the Beatles since the beginning, driving them from concert to concert in his van, getting paid next to nothing. But now the big executive bucks weren't enough to satisfy him. He was sick of taking everybody's shit. If it was going to continue, he wanted to be set for life.

John was outraged, because if Neil got more, he got less. But there was still no way he was going to that meeting at the Plaza. The last time he had gone was 1975, and afterward he vowed to never go again. They sat for hours bickering over nonsense. Everybody, it seemed, was hell-bent on frustrating everybody else, just for the sheer pleasure of it. Since each decision required unanimous approval, frustration was easy.

John, to amuse himself, had sat there scribbling notes, scrawling cartoons. When it was over, nothing had changed, and only two things were certain: they were going to do it again in three months, and he was not going to be there. He had enough frustration to contend with; he didn't need to go looking for more. He didn't even want the others to see him. It was better to be a phantom.

Neil called John the day before the January 1980 meeting to say he was confident that all would go well. Lennon knew that meant Neil was worried. But John was more worried—he was a nervous wreck.

The next day Yoko went to the Plaza Hotel to play her game of mortal combat with the Apples. John, in a state of intense anxiety, waited in his bedroom, counting the hours. Finally, Yoko returned with news that made him jubilant and proved the horoscope correct: she got her way. The Apple money would continue to flow in rivers and oceans. John praised the Lord for giving Yoko the power to always get her way. *Thank You. Thank You. Thank You.*

MONEY

THERE WAS NO REAL REASON FOR JOHN AND YOKO TO subject themselves to this annual Apple agony. They could have walked away and never looked back. They *did* have too much money. Barring a total collapse of the global economy, they had enough real estate, livestock, art, antiques, collectibles, stocks, bonds, precious metals, and cash to survive any calamity, continue living exactly as they'd been living, and insure that unborn generations would want for nothing. Their life had become an endless shopping spree. They were incapable of so much as walking into a supermarket without blowing six-hundred dollars, which invariably raised the question, *Who is going to eat all this food?*

The Lennons had grown accustomed to a lifestyle of seemingly unlimited resources. The one overindulgence John never chastised himself for was spending too much money.

Yet no amount of money was ever enough for the Lennons, because they were bound together by a gnawing emptiness that money could never fill. The root of John's pain was his father's desertion when he was five years old and his mother's death when he was 17—experiences so traumatic, he'd never fully recovered. Once he had believed that unlimited doses of money and fame would stop the pain. By the time he discovered that money and fame actually exacerbated it, leaving him addicted to more money and more fame, he was too far gone to ever be helped. LSD couldn't save him. The Maharishi couldn't save him. Leaving the Beatles couldn't save him. Primal therapy couldn't save him. And Yoko, who shared his addictions, certainly couldn't save him.

Outside of heroin, the only thing that seemed to momentarily alleviate the Lennons' pain was the instantaneous gratification of a $100,000 shopping expedition. But the pain always returned, and

each time it did, it hurt a little bit worse, with the emptiness growing a little bigger.

It had certainly crossed John's mind to give everything away,
but that was never going to happen. Money was identity, and without it John and Yoko would cease to exist. They wouldn't be able
to sit around all day, stewing in their misery and consulting their
psychics. They'd have to work...or live in a monastery, and that was
unacceptable.

Maintaining The Myth of John and Yoko was also a very expensive proposition. In May 1979, when they felt that The Myth was
starting to fray around the edges, it took $60,000—chump change
by their standards—to buy full-page ads in *The New York Times, The
Times of London* and a major Tokyo daily to reaffirm it. That was
their "Love Letter to the People." "The plants are growing and the
cats are purring," they said, assuring the world that there was nothing to worry about. They were happy, their magic was real and everything was under control. That was all anybody needed to know.

They weren't lying; The Myth of John and Yoko was real, but
only in brief, ecstatic flashes. And those flashes had been growing
progressively more infrequent. Like moments of a dream, when
they ended, it was as if they'd never happened. Only when John
wrote about them did the moments become real to him. Words
were reality, and John's reality was boredom and pain punctuated
by microseconds of ecstasy. Buried alive in a high-rent purgatory of
superstition and fear, he often wondered if something good was
ever going to happen to him again, or if it was just going to go on
like this till the day he died. John and Yoko shared a mutual dread
of the world learning how bad it had become for them.

If Yoko ever had to begin auctioning off her priceless Egyptian
antiques or selling her Dakota apartments, people might begin to
suspect that all was not well in Nutopia, the imaginary country
without laws, land or boundaries that the Lennons had whimsically
founded in 1973.

*Are they running out of money? Are they coming apart at the
seams like the rest of us?*

Though some might have dimly imagined the true nature of life
at the Dakota, most people still accepted The Myth at face value,
and those who didn't were probably on the payroll. And if most

people perceived The Myth as reality, then it *was* reality. That was magic, and that was what John and Yoko believed.

The only problem with this magical theory was the growing number of people not currently on the payroll who had done business with Yoko and learned the truth the hard way. Her business philosophy was based on the three rules she learned from dealing with Apple: 1) There are no rules. 2) Lawyers are everything; contracts are nothing. 3) Everybody gets burned.

Yoko, dressed in the robes of The High Priestess, had become a New Age capitalist monster. She and John had gotten more than their share of money. They had made too many enemies who wanted to take away their money. And if these people couldn't get their money, then they were going to find some way to make John and Yoko miserable. And the easiest way to do that was with lawsuits. Somebody was always suing or threatening to sue. John walked the streets seeing in the shadows men with subpoenas. Yet he clung to the belief that in the end it would all work out: Yoko *was* a money magician. Even if Apple somehow managed to cut them off completely and everything they owned was destroyed by fire, Yoko had the power to transform a cat turd into a lump of gold.

Yoko certainly understood the value of a dollar—at least when it came to other people. In 1979 she sent one of her Japanese nephews to work for concert promoter Norman Seaman, the husband of Sean's governess, Helen. Seaman told the kid to stand on a street corner and distribute promotional flyers. He was going to pay him $3.50 per hour, which was below minimum wage. Yoko forbade it.

"Pay him one dollar per hour," she told Seaman. "I want him to learn the value of money."

John and Yoko wanted everybody to understand how valuable *their* money was. And they also wanted everybody to understand that it was their money, to do with as they pleased, when they pleased. This attitude didn't do much for their social life. The only friends they had were each other, and that was the way they wanted it. Friends meant obligations and responsibilities, and they already had enough of those. John had learned a long time ago that he could never have any real friends—people who would accept him for being himself, who wouldn't care whether he was a millionaire or pauper, a superstar or anonymous. But how could anybody accept him for being himself when, beyond multimillionaire ex-Beatle, he didn't have a clue as to who he was.

John and Yoko had more of everything than anybody else they knew, except for Paul and Linda McCartney, and even that was debatable. The problem with having more of everything was that everybody they knew wanted something from them; they expected it. Inevitably, they demanded it: *"Gimme!"* John hated that. He didn't need close personal friends to make demands on him. The whole world was his close personal friend and everybody wanted a piece of the action. No need to encourage them.

Having no friends was freedom. When John needed company, he bought it. That was the beauty of servants. When he was feeling generally disgusted, there was always somebody around more than willing to listen to him primal. A few actually had brains. He talked "at" them and they appeared to understand. They responded intelligently, sympathetically—not that he cared how they responded. Sometimes he opened up completely and got it all off his chest. Sean's nanny was a great audience; Helen stimulated John to wax philosophical, and he primalled in front of her all the time. When the urge struck him, he could be a "quagmire of monologue," as he described himself in *Skywriting By Word of Mouth*. Out of the blue he'd say stuff to Helen like, "All the great ones, all the artists and scientists and psychics and musicians and philosophers—they were all bloody mystics! Fuckin' Einstein said as much: If he had it to do over, he'd have spent more time working on his spiritual side. Buddha and Beethoven and Browning and Balzac and Blake and Byron and Brahms and especially Jesus Bloody Christ—mystics all! Pythagoras and Picasso! Mohammed and Mozart! Krishna and Kafka and Kierkegaard! Newton and Nabokov and Nijinsky! They're all fuckin' mystics and seers. They understood, to receive the muse you've got to empty your mind! You can't bloody well paint a picture on a dirty piece of paper, now can you?"

When he got tired of talking at Helen, he'd send her away. The servants might not particularly enjoy being treated like objects, but that was their job, which they were being well paid for, and they'd better not forget it.

The closest thing John and Yoko had to friends were the actor Peter Boyle and his wife, Lorraine Alterman. They hung out with the Lennons more than anybody who wasn't on the payroll.

John knew Peter wanted something from him, even though Peter did a better job of hiding it than most people. John found him amusing, Lorraine interesting. He rarely felt threatened by them. It was easy for John to feel superior to Peter. The Boyles understood their place and made few demands. To be known as John and Yoko's buddies was reward enough.

Lorraine, a former gossip journalist who had worked for *Rolling Stone*, was well connected to the celebrity set. She'd known Yoko for years. Before marrying Peter in 1975, she'd drop by the Dakota to swap gossip with John and Yoko. She was also a good cook, and on rare occasions the Lennons would attend one of her gala dinner parties.

John looked upon all social gatherings as drinks, drugs and bullshit and tried to avoid them whenever possible. He knew that if Lorraine knew he was coming to dinner, she'd go all out to make it a celebrity gathering of the first magnitude. That was the kind of scene John hated and feared. He felt pressured to live up to his legend.

Lorraine was friendly with Paul Simon, and John knew that she wanted to get them together. But John despised Simon. His name alone—Paul—was enough to give him the creeps. Simon's lyrics and voice made John sick to his stomach. He was also insanely jealous of Simon's unabated success and had developed a wicked impersonation that he performed for his servants when the mood struck him. He'd refer to the singer as a twerp.

The real problem between the two superstars dated back to May 1974. Simon, along with his old partner, Art Garfunkel, had shown up at a recording session in New York's Record Plant for Harry Nilsson's *Pussy Cats* LP, which John was producing. The pop duo were there because they wanted to work with Lennon. They kept trying to harmonize behind Nilsson, but they hadn't sung together in four years and kept messing up. Cues were missed. Take after take was ruined. Though Lennon remained professionally stoic through the ordeal, Nilsson lost his cool and began screaming at Simon and Garfunkel. Then Garfunkel and Simon started screaming at each other. Lennon was disgusted by the scene and lost what little respect for Simon he had.

But John was quite impressed with Lorraine. He liked the fact that she was a close friend of Danny Kaye. He liked Danny Kaye. In June 1975, John had performed on a television show, *Salute to Lew Grade*. When John showed up with Yoko at the studio, he realized there had been a mistake. They had the wrong Beatle; they had wanted Paul to sing. Everybody in the place was giving him bad vibes and he was giving them back. Then he went onstage and, as he described it later, "spat *Imagine* at them." The audience reception was icy. Backstage, the only person who acknowledged him was Danny Kaye, with a big thumbs-up.

John also respected and feared Lorraine because she was friends with Paul and Linda McCartney.

After Peter and Lorraine married, there were the inevitable squabbles and misunderstandings. After a fight, Lorraine would go to Yoko for comfort, and Peter would end up with John, seeking solace about his career troubles. But mostly the relationship between the two couples consisted of eating dinner at chic Soho restaurants of Peter's choosing. He was perpetually discovering hot new eateries that John detested. The food was always greasy and always gave him indigestion. The service was always bad. And it always cost a small fortune. He never had a good word for Peter's choice of restaurants. When it came to food, he thought Peter didn't have a clue. But he continued to let Peter pick the restaurants because he got too much pleasure out of criticizing him for his lack of taste.

And that was worth the money.

HIS FINEST HOUR

JOHN LENNON AND PAUL MCCARTNEY WERE ONCE the best of friends, drawn together as teenagers by a love of rock 'n' roll and the pain from the death of their mothers. But by 1980 the animosity that had developed between them had reached absurd proportions. They were empires at war—a war that had raged virtually unabated for over ten years, since the day in 1969 when John, on the advice of Mick Jagger, chose Allen Klein as his business manager and Paul chose his father-in-law, John Eastman.

They had fought bloody battles face-to-face at conference tables. They had plundered each other with lawyers, wounded each other with music. Propaganda warfare raged in the media. In

AP/Wide World Photos

Allen Klein discusses a contract with John Lennon and Yoko Ono in January 1977. Paul McCartney never forgave Lennon for choosing Klein as his business manager instead of McCartney's father-in-law, John Eastman.

moments of desperation John had resorted to witchcraft and black magic. Ceasefires broke down. Moments of truce at dinner tables erupted into vicious psychological combat. If they had had The Bomb, they'd have nuked each other back to the Stone Age. There was no rational reason for the slaughter. It was a war of irreconcilable ideological differences—and jealously.

It drove John bonkers that while he'd gone five years with no public acclaim, Paul had continued to pump out hit after hit, perpetually riding high on the charts. Paul, not John, was the most successful ex-Beatle...and he had a bigger family, too. Paul was happier!

John saw himself as a paranoid ex-Beatle walking the streets of New York City. He was forever trying to escape a Beatle past that was impossible to escape. Paul, more than anything, represented that past. McCartney's constant demands for a Beatles reunion genuinely repulsed John. Paul, he felt, basically hadn't changed in 25 years.

During a brief period in 1976, Paul would sometimes show up unannounced at the Dakota. The "old charmer" would talk his way past the security guard and knock on John's door. John would open up and there would be Paul, standing there smiling, guitar in hand. Occasionally Linda came with him.

John tolerated it for a while. He even enjoyed the company. They'd hang out and watch TV. Usually though, John was exhausted

AP/Wide World Photos

John Lennon and Paul McCartney announce the creation of Apple Corps, Ltd., at a New York news conference, March 1968. Intended as a utopian business venture, Apple instead marked the beginning of the end of the Beatles and drove John and Paul to new heights of animosity.

from a long day with Sean. Eventually he began to resent the unexpected intrusions.

"It's not like we're 17 years old anymore," John told him. "Next time call before you come."

"Are you telling me to fuck off?" Paul asked.

"If that's the way you want to put it, then fuck off."

That marked the end of one ceasefire. John had always loved Paul like a brother; he just couldn't stand being around him.

They saw each other again in 1977. The McCartneys and Lennons ate dinner together at Le Cirque, Paul's favorite French restaurant in New York. John regretted going; it was a loathsome night. Paul and Linda blathered on and on about how perfect their lives were, how they had everything they'd ever wanted, and how they were as happy as they'd ever been.

Something very paranoid suddenly occurred to John. Maybe Lorraine Boyle was spying on him for the McCartneys!

He woke up the next morning still feeling disturbed; he consulted the Oracle. Swan assured him that Paul and Linda were frustrated and unsatisfied. Their marriage was in trouble, he said, predicting it would break up within the year. Lately Swan's visions had been astonishingly accurate. Relieved, John began composing a song—a little ditty, really, that would never be released—in praise of the Oracle's powers. But he still couldn't understand why Paul and Linda had been together for as long as they had.

There appeared to be a psychic connection between John and Paul. Every time McCartney was in town, John would hear Paul's music in his head.

There was a McCartney symphony playing in John's head when Paul, en route to Japan with his band Wings, called the afternoon of January 14, 1980, from the Stanhope Hotel on Fifth Avenue in New York. He'd scored some excellent weed, he told John, and offered to stop by the Dakota to give him a taste.

"No thanks," Lennon replied.

McCartney then mentioned that in Tokyo, he intended to stay in the Okura Hotel's Presidential Suite.

John freaked. He and Yoko had always stayed in the Okura's Presidential Suite, and he considered it their private suite. The idea of Paul and Linda sleeping in their bed made John physically ill. He was convinced the "McEastmans" would ruin his hotel karma.

To calm himself he transformed a *New Yorker* cartoon of a woman at the complaint counter of a department store into a cartoon of himself, Yoko, and Sean filing a complaint against the McCartneys at the Okura desk.

There was only one thing to do, Yoko said. Using the magic she'd learned three years earlier from Lena the Columbian Witch, she would curse the McCartneys.

Yes, John agreed, it *had* to be done.

John's finest hour of the new year came on January 16, when he received word that Paul had been busted at Tokyo International Airport with eight ounces of marijuana. The news was enough to momentarily take Lennon's mind off his own misery. Euphoric, he could hardly believe that Paul was having a worse day than he was.

John, convinced that Yoko had used her occult powers to bring about the arrest, gave her full credit for the deed. Delighting in the thought of Paul behind bars where he belonged, John praised the Lord: *Thank You. Thank You. Thank You.* He knew it was absurd and childish to only see his life as being better or worse than McCartney's, but he couldn't help himself, and for the time being he was going to enjoy it thoroughly.

Paul was released ten days later. John was disappointed that they didn't keep him locked up a bit longer. But he took solace in the fact that McCartney was expelled from Japan, the Wings tour was cancelled, and millions of dollars were down the drain. Paul had it coming to him, and John had known that it was only a matter of time before he got it.

PEOPLE I
REMEMBER

IT WASN'T ALWAYS LIKE THIS.

Something fundamental had changed for John during his years of seclusion. Back in 1975, life was as it should have been. He was making music and trying to join the musician's union. He was laughing raucously at Howard Cosell's absurd suggestion that the Beatles should reunite on his show. He was doing his liveliest, most coherent writing. And his fun wasn't even diminished by the fact that two of the people he was constantly dealing with were Harold Seider and Morris Levy. The former was his business advisor and attorney, who was urging him to sign the papers that would at last dissolve the Beatles partnership. The latter was a music publisher with whom he was involved in an extremely messy series of legal disputes having to do with plagiarism, broken promises, and reneged deals. One lawsuit resulted from the simultaneous release by Levy's company and Capitol Records of the same album under two different names, *Roots* and *Rock 'n' Roll*. *Roots* was being sold on TV like a cheesy golden oldie before Levy was forced to withdraw the LP.

As 1974 ended, John had just returned to New York from winter vacation in California and Florida with Julian, who was then 11, and May Pang, his mistress and former secretary. Father and son were ensconced in May's East Side apartment. John was suffering from a mild head cold and what seemed like terminal constipation. Mostly, he sat in bed with a cat curled up at his feet, blowing his nose and watching TV.

The next week, John, recovered, spent his afternoons with Julian, walking around New York, shopping. To insure anonymity, they wore ski masks. One afternoon while walking on Fifth Avenue, they stopped to watch a man pounding on the doors of a church.

The man was screaming to be let inside but the doors were locked. "Does the Lord not live here?" the man cried. John shouted his encouragement and kept walking towards FAO Schwartz, the famous toy store, where Julian would be turned loose.

During this period in early 1975, while living with May, John was also spending time with Mick Jagger, just as they had in the mid-60's in London. Lennon still liked Jagger. Jagger had not yet made the offhand remark to the British press—"You can't have a career and a family"—that John felt was directed at him and that he considered slanderous. He'd not yet begun to call the Rolling Stone "Mick Faggot." (Nor had he begun to call Paul McCartney "McAsshole.")

His other *mate* was David Bowie. The previous year, John had done Bowie the tremendous favor of playing guitar on his *Young Americans* album, and had co-written *Fame,* Bowie's first number one hit. Now Bowie was making a bit of a nuisance of himself, always calling on the phone, inviting himself over and trying to drag John out to rock concerts. Lennon was reluctant to see other bands, but he did allow Bowie to take him to Madison Square Garden to check out Julian's favorite group, Led Zeppelin. Although he dismissed the group as ordinary, the next day Lennon was amazed to hear Julian picking out on a guitar the opening chords of *Stairway to Heaven.*

One night Bowie and Jagger dropped by unannounced at May's apartment with Todd Rundgren's gorgeous, 20-year-old wife, Bebe Buell, a model and *Playboy* "playmate." It was an awkward situation. At the time, Lennon and Rundgren were feuding publicly in the pages of the British weekly music magazine *Melody Maker.* Rundgren had criticized Lennon in an interview, falsely accusing him, among other things, of punching out a waitress in L.A.'s Troubadour Club. This was a reference to the legendary night the previous year that Lennon, who had had far too much to drink, was heckling the Smothers Brothers and stumbling around the club with a Kotex on his head. "Do you know who I am?" he had asked the waitress.

"An asshole with a Kotex on your head," she had replied.

Lennon responded to Rundgren's accusation with a letter to the editor. "I never hit a waitress in the Troubadour," he wrote. "I did act like an ass, I was too drunk. So shoot me!" He also called him "Turd Runtgreen."

Apparently, Bebe did not hold this against Lennon. (She'd soon divorce Rundgren.) When she walked out of the room for a few minutes, Mick told John that he was planning on having sex with her. This made John feel insecure and more than a little jealous. Then Mick took out some drugs. John didn't even ask what they were. He just snorted a bit of the white powder, got violently ill and passed out.

Bowie called the next day to see how John was.

"Could be better," Lennon answered.

Bowie told John that he and Jagger had gone to Harlem and had had a blast wandering around in the wee hours of the morning. John thought they were nuts, and was glad that he'd gotten sick. Otherwise he'd have ended up going with them and probably getting into unimaginable trouble.

The next night was far more subdued. John, May and Julian sat in the living room watching *A Hard Day's Night* on TV. John couldn't believe that ten years had passed since he made the film.

John was torn between May and Yoko. He wanted both of them, but that was out of the question. May was fun, and pure sexual passion. When he was with her, he was content. Yoko, though, was survival. John occasionally met with her to talk of reconciliation. But every time they got together, she'd play all kinds of freaky emotional games and try to pressure him to come home.

That's why John spent most of his time in bed with May, making love. It was his last taste of sexual bliss. They devoted their days to fucking and sucking and jacking each other off. In between they'd sleep for a few hours. Then they'd wake up and do it again ...and again.

Even after he went home to Mother, John pined for May until the day he died, constantly repressing the urge to call her. He made no effort to hide from Yoko the fact that running back to May was always on his mind. It infuriated her.

But John stayed with Yoko because he loved her and needed her, and because she was the mother of his child. There was really no choice. Existence in the Dakota might have been living death, but existence outside the Dakota was unthinkable. John believed Yoko was his last and only hope to save himself from himself, and as long as he had her, something better was always near. It was only a matter of time.

Part II

GETTING CENTERED

INTERLUDE AT
EL SALANO

THE LENNONS WERE DETERMINED TO BUY A FEW
mansions, and they'd spent five years looking for suitable
estates. In November 1979, after having inspected scores of exclusive properties in Westchester County, New York; Ontario, Canada;
the state of Maine; and just about every place else in between, they
still hadn't found anything they liked.

John and Yoko never actually looked at the properties. That
would freak people out and drive up the price. Instead, they dispatched a servant to take Polaroid pictures. The servant would tell
the real estate agent that he represented a businessman who preferred to remain anonymous. Yoko would then study the pictures
with her Council of Seers. There was always a problem: The property wasn't secluded enough. Or the Oracle, after a tarot reading,
advised against buying it. Or Yoko picked up bad vibrations from
the photographs. Or the house faced in the wrong direction according to the laws of feng shui, or it had bad numbers.

Then they found Cannon Hill, in Cold Spring Harbor, Long
Island, only an hour's drive from the Dakota. Thus began a real
estate buying binge.

"You will acquire property," said the O after reading on Cannon
Hill many times.

John and Yoko, agreeing his vision was clear and true, shelled
out $450,000 for the house. It had 14 bedrooms and a wood-
shingled mansard roof. The backyard, which included a swimming
pool and a gazebo, overlooked Long Island Sound. John loved
Cannon Hill. It was the house of his dreams.

Two months later, they decided to buy *El Salano*, the Palm
Beach, Florida, oceanfront estate they'd rented the previous spring
for $300,000.

It came complete with a sauna, six master bedrooms, five servant rooms, a tennis court, an indoor freshwater pool, an outdoor saltwater pool, and a pool cabana with a bath and teahouse. For over 60 years the Spanish-style mansion had been the scene of the city's most spectacular social gatherings. The Vanderbilt family had once lived here. Rose Kennedy had recently attended an El Salano party in her honor. Douglas Fairbanks, Jr., and Nicholas DuPont had frolicked at El Salano. Even *Hustler* publisher Larry Flynt had rented the property, and outraged the neighbors by using it for porno shoots.

At one million dollars, it was a steal! But they had to act quickly. January was coming to an end, and the stars said that it was the best month for matters pertaining to resources and long-term security.

The numbers, too, were perfect. The address, 720 South Ocean Boulevard: 9. The name, El Salano: 10 or 1, the ideal complement to 9 as well as the number of the sun, the source of light, the tarot symbol of all that is creative and positive.

Yoko closed the deal on January 27, and John praised the Lord for granting him a beautiful piece of Florida Gold Coast real estate—*Thank You! Thank You! Thank You!*

By the time he and Sean settled into El Salano in early February with a small retinue of servants, John had fallen in love with the house. He drew a big, radiant sun smiling contentedly on his ocean.

Even on cloudy days, when the sky and the ocean were gunmetal gray, every sun John drew was a happy sun. Suddenly, all seemed well. Maybe it was just the gloomy Dakota and the oppressive New York City winter that had had him feeling down. In "God's Waiting Room," as Palm Beach is called, he could breathe again.

In the morning, the sun rose over the ocean. As light poured through the enormous picture window, flooding the living room and filling him with energy, John sat in a club chair reading *The Palm Beach Post*. It pleased him enormously that an article on page one of the Leisure section reported that he and Yoko had just bought El Salano. The wire services would pick up the story, and McCartney was bound to see it.

John didn't care that spending money was the only way he could make headlines anymore. Every headline was a psychic victory over

Paul, and this was a million dollar headline. He gloated thinking of Paul's jealousy. McCartney had gotten out of jail just two weeks ago. He imagined him in seclusion at his sheep farm in Scotland, still shaken by the Japanese fiasco. Yes, John thought, 1980 is going to be the magnificent year the O has forecast. Soon he was going to be centered; soon he was going to make even more money.

Money! Money! Money! It was the crux of everything. Who was richer, Lennon or McCartney? That was the question that haunted John.

When a second article, which estimated the Lennon fortune at $150 million, appeared in *The Palm Beach Post,* John clipped it. He was richer than McCartney now—he was certain of it—and an old cliché flitted across his brain: *To live well is the best revenge.*

John understood better than most people how destructive it was to think about money all the time. It was not the way to get centered, which was what he was supposed to be doing in Florida. He knew he had to find a more productive way to channel his energy.

Every morning John and Sean rose with the sun. Sometimes John put Sean into a safety seat mounted on the rear fender of his bicycle and took him riding on a path by the ocean. Other mornings they walked along the beach. It was cold for February and John was a little disappointed. He wanted the weather to be perfect. One morning they met an old man who lived down the road. Realizing that the man had no idea who he was, John told him that he'd just moved to Palm Beach. The old man apologized for the weather, explaining that it was the coldest February on record.

By the end of the week, John had begun playing the guitar and piano. Sean sat on the living room floor, listening to him. Feeling nostalgic, John donned the gaucho costume he wore on the cover of *Hey Jude.* He sat in the club chair strumming his guitar, his life a movie.

Early one morning two adolescent boys knocked on the door, and John answered it, as he sometimes did.

"Does John Lennon live here?" one of them asked.

"No," said John, closing the door.

He was in no mood for such intrusion. Real fans would have recognized him immediately; they'd have reacted as if Jesus Bloody Christ had opened the door. The boys, he suspected, had been sent by their parents to get an autograph. Had they been sincere he'd have let them in, chatted for a few moments. Recently, one of the neighbors' kids at the Dakota had knocked on the door and Lennon had told his astonished servant to let the boy in. He sat with the kid in the kitchen for a good half hour, answering his questions about life and fame and the Beatles. He was into it. He wanted to share his knowledge, enlighten the boy, show him the way.

Now he just wanted his serenity, to sit by the window in the living room with the newspaper, drinking his first cup of black coffee, smoking his first Gitane.

By the week of February 11, the weather had improved, the sun burning away the clouds and turning the ocean a Carribean shade of turquoise. The afternoons were now sweltering. Yoko, wanting to be with John and Sean for her birthday, flew to Palm Beach. But as soon as she arrived, she said that they had to be back in New York no later than the 25th, before the onset of Mercury Retrograde, which would make travel impossible.

Yoko had taught John everything he needed to know about Mercury Retrograde, the times of year when the planet Mercury appears to move backwards in the sky and for three weeks it's as if Murphy's law has been written in the stars: everything that can go wrong will go wrong. John hated and feared these tri-annual episodes as much as Yoko did, or at least he pretended to. As Mercury Retrograde neared, he'd count down the days, then try to deal with it as best he could according to Mother's rules of astrology, tarot, and numerology.

As far as Yoko was concerned, when Mercury Retrograde kicked in, the only thing to do was nothing, preferably in a house that faced in the right direction. You can't fight Mercury Retrograde. Nothing will be accomplished. The best way to deal with it is to anticipate it, plan your year around it. And Yoko just wanted to make sure that when it happened, they weren't trapped in Palm Beach, a thousand miles from New York City.

But he still had two more weeks to enjoy his subtropical paradise, and John planned on milking all the pleasure he could from every second of every day.

THE VISITORS

JOHN PLAYED THE PIANO FOR YOKO HER FIRST EVENING in Palm Beach. They spent the next afternoon by the outdoor pool. John and Sean loved to swim, but Yoko didn't. Wearing an orange terry cloth cabana outfit and sun visor, she sat in a beach chair in the fetal position, watching them.

Sometimes in the morning John and Yoko, hiding under hats and behind sunglasses, walked along the beach. Once, a reporter spotted them and demanded an interview.

"I don't do interviews," John told him. "I haven't done interviews in five years."

A picture of them walking on the beach, holding hands, appeared in the local paper. They were pleased.

Two items in the February 14 edition of *The Palm Beach Post* caught John's attention. The first article, on page three of the Leisure section—"British Medium: Spiritualism in an Upsurge"—told of Mollie Moncrieff, a spirit channeller who had developed an interest in theosophy after her mother's death. Through mediums she was able to communicate with her dead uncle George, who assured her that her mother's spirit was doing well in the great beyond. Moncrieff was in Palm Beach to give a series of lectures about the ancient wisdom of the East and about applying information gleaned from your past lives to your present life.

John was intrigued, and for a fleeting moment considered going to a lecture, but thought better of it.

Turning the page, he was struck by the headline "Reclusive Brando Gives Funeral Dramatic Aura." The article was a description of the 300-pound Marlon Brando being swarmed by paparazzi as he emerged from a Beverly Hills church after Jimmy Durante's funeral. It said: *Here was a heavy-set man, plodding along in a winking, flashing, brilliant pool of strobe lights, surrounded on all sides by dark, face-*

less creatures with cameras, most of them young and agile. One imme-diately thought of an old lion beset by jackals closing in for the kill.

John pondered fame and the inevitability of death, and it gave him a chill.

Later in the week, Peter and Lorraine Boyle came to El Salano. Everybody sat by the outdoor pool, with Uda-San serving them food and drink. John strummed his guitar. Peter danced around, like a jester. But from the moment he arrived, he got on John's nerves. Peter wanted to go out, do the town, be seen with John. John refused. The last time he'd agreed to go out, the Boyles had dragged him to Lincoln Center to see the classical ballet *Swan Lake*. It was a dreadful night of boredom and autograph hounds.

But Peter continued to press the issue, and John, against his better judgement, relented.

The night of the outing, Yoko wore a pure white dress and looked like a bride. John, his hair tied back in a ponytail, wore his "space suit": white pants, white shirt, black jacket and Quarry Bank school tie. A servant took snapshots of John, Yoko, Peter and Lorraine. Then they were transported by limousine to La Petite Marmite, an exclusive Worth Avenue Restaurant. As soon as they stepped out of the limo, the paparazzi were on them; strobes explod-ed. Their dinner was constantly interrupted by people demanding autographs. But Peter got exactly what he wanted—he was seen in public and photographed with John. Now he'd have to pay the price.

Back at El Salano, in front of the servants, John began to viciously provoke Peter.

"You're dumb," he said.

"Don't call me dumb!" Peter shouted. "I'm not dumb! And you can go fuck yourself!" Then he began crying.

John was delighted that he'd driven Peter over the edge and into a primal state. He felt emotionally and spiritually superior. Then, bored with the mind games, he sent the Boyles home.

H A P P Y   B I R T H D A Y
D E A R   Y O K O

YOKO TURNED 47 ON FEBRUARY 18. SHE WAS depressed and depressing to be around, again sitting silently by the pool in the fetal position.

John had always gone to great lengths to please Yoko on her birthday. Three years ago, he had worked every day for a solid month in a Soho artist's studio putting together a collage for her. But as it neared completion, he fell into despair. The collage wasn't bad, he thought, but it wasn't great either, and he dreaded giving Yoko a mediocre birthday present.

This time John and Sean attempted to transcend mediocrity by showering Yoko with a fur coat, 150 gardenias, and a tinkling bell. But Mother barely cracked a smile, perhaps because, unbeknownst to John, gardenias are a Japanese symbol of death.

John then suggested a shopping spree, and that did make Yoko happy. She went to Saks and in less than an hour spent $17,000 on clothing. There was no place to put it all, so the next day they bought two-thousand dollars' worth of storage trunks.

IMAGINE

DRIVING BY A MARINA IN PALM BEACH, JOHN SPOTTED a sleek powerboat called Imagine. Taking it as an omen, he had his assistant charter the yacht for an afternoon.

The captain and his wife, the first mate, were aging flower children and were naturally astonished to have the Lennon family aboard. The captain confessed to John that during an LSD trip many years ago, he'd gotten the inspiration to name the boat Imagine.

Cool, John thought.

Sean had a blast out on the ocean, scampering around the deck, playing with a cat, saluting the American flag, and sitting in the captain's chair, steering. Food was served, and it was delicious. Everybody ate but Yoko, who was still brooding over God knows what, and now getting seasick, too. Nobody could do anything to cheer her up. She hid behind her sunglasses and her big, drooping straw hat. As the ubiquitous assistant snapped pictures, Yoko continued brooding. Then John put his arms around her. She cracked a smile for the camera, which made John happy because this was how he wanted the world to see them.

JUDE

SOON AFTER YOKO'S BIRTHDAY, JULIAN CALLED JOHN AT EL Salano from Ruthin, Wales, where he lived with his mother, Cynthia, and asked to come to Palm Beach for a few weeks. John thought about the previous April, when Julian had come for his sixteenth birthday. John hadn't seen him since early 1975, when they had stayed together at May Pang's apartment. Far too much time had passed between visits, and John knew he could never let it happen again.

He had been nervous before Julian's arrival that previous spring. He paced by the pool, strumming his guitar. A *New Yorker* cartoon prompted him to wonder if his son would even recognize him. In the cartoon, a man looked in the mirror, contemplating changing his appearance, holding a comb under his nose to represent a moustache. "They'll never recognize me," said the caption. John transformed the man into himself by adding a ponytail and glasses. On the opposite page was a cartoon of a man being knighted. "I dub thee sir nice guy," said that caption. This character, too, John transformed into himself. It embodied one of his more humble ambitions—to be recognized as a nice guy.

As it turned out, Julian and John got along better than John had expected. The change in Julian was dramatic. He'd been through a lot, and it showed. Julian now wanted to be a drummer in a rock band, and John understood how difficult it would be for his son to live up to the Lennon name. Already people teased him every time he picked up a guitar. *Fuckin' Lennon, ya play like fuckin' dogshit.* But Julian was strong, and the taunting didn't deter him.

Nineteen seventy-nine was the first time that John, Yoko, Julian and Sean were together in the same house. John was overjoyed and thought that someday maybe they could all live together permanently. But deep down he knew that it would never happen. He

AP/Wide World Photos

Paul McCartney and John Lennon arrive in Athens,
Greece, July 1967. Paul, accompanied by his girlfriend,
actress Jane Asher (left), holds the hand of Julian
Lennon. A year later Paul would write Hey Jude for
Julian to cheer him up after John divorced Julian's
mother, Cynthia. John and Julian were never close, and
their inability to connect remained a source of anguish
for both of them throughout their lives.

knew that Julian resented Yoko and would always hold her responsible for breaking up his marriage with Cynthia. Yoko knew it too; when she tried to reach out to Julian, she was coldly rebuffed.

One night Yoko and Julian sat at the kitchen table. She was trying to teach him the Japanese art of origami, intricately folding sheets of paper into various animal shapes. Julian sat patiently, watching Yoko, pretending to be interested. But polite was the best he could do. Julian was incapable of acting warmly towards his stepmother. He made it clear that he was in Palm Beach to be with his father and brother. After the origami session, Julian wrestled with

Sean on the living room floor. In the morning, John, Julian and Sean went bike riding.

Later that week the Richter children came to visit. Their father, Dan Richter, was an old friend of John and Yoko's. He was famous for his role as the "Ape with the Idea" in the opening scene of Stanley Kubrick's *2001,* and he'd worked with John and Yoko on Yoko's experimental film *Fly.*

The kids played musical chairs, with John supplying live guitar music.

Julian had come to Palm Beach equipped with lifelike rubber masks and rubber reptiles. He wore the masks all the time, even at the dinner table. His favorite was an old man mask, which he liked to wear in the street.

Three of Yoko's "Japan-nieces," one of whom was Julian's age, flew in from Tokyo, and everybody went to Disney World. They all wore Julian's masks and dragged around on leashes his two-foot-long iguanas and crocodiles.

April 4 was Julian's sixteenth birthday. In the morning, a man and woman, dressed in tuxedos, appeared at the front door and sang "Happy Birthday."

John was moved by the idea that his son, who had now formally declared that he wanted to be a rock musician, had reached the age when it had all begun to happen for him.

That afternoon John, Yoko, Sean, Julian, and the Japan-nieces went out on a chartered yacht. John and Julian sat alone in the front of the boat, talking. John tried to explain what had happened all those years ago with Yoko and Cynthia. He assured Julian that he did love him, and in the future they'd be closer than ever, but it would be a long, difficult process. It was the first time John had ever tried to explain any of this to his son. Julian nodded, acting as if he understood. John said that they could never again let four years pass between visits.

The next day Julian went back to Ruthin with a load of presents. John was unhappy to see him go. But the visit had been stressful, and in a way it was a relief to say goodbye. It was exactly how he felt in 1975 when he sent Julian back to England with a load of gifts.

Julian would never see his father again.

When he called in February 1980 wanting to come to Palm Beach, John said no—for Julian's own good. Julian had his "O-levels" coming up; these were the exams he needed to pass to graduate from high school. Since the beginning of the year, John had been praying for Julian to pass.

Twenty-three years ago, John had failed all his O-levels because he didn't give a fuck, because he didn't need a diploma to be a musician. He was afraid that Julian was going to drop out of school as he had dropped out of school—to pursue rock 'n' roll.

"You have plenty of time to become a musician," he assured his son. "Your circumstances are completely different than mine. You don't *need* to become a musician to survive. Stay in Ruthin and study. Education is important."

Julian was doing poorly in school, passing by the skin of his teeth. John knew that the only reason Julian wasn't failing everything was because his name was Lennon and the teachers were being kind. Cynthia had already told him that Julian had taken up smoking cigarettes and that he was staying out nights drinking. He'd also gotten into trouble with the police, setting fires and racing recklessly through town on a dirt bike. But the cops always let him go because he was John Lennon's son, the spitting image of his father, and they dimly understood the sort of pressure he was under.

John just prayed that Julian didn't hurt himself.

Like his father, Julian didn't give a fuck about school. He was looking for an excuse to drop out, take his chances. School bored him to death; he wasn't learning anything. When he finally did take his O-levels, he failed abysmally. Most of his marks were in the teens; his highest mark was 42—on a scale of 100. The news depressed John. When he called Julian on his seventeenth birthday, Julian told him that he'd been out all night drinking. John took it in stride.

Then Julian asked him for more money. Every time John spoke to Julian, Julian asked him for more money. The only thing Julian wanted from him, John feared, was more money. And though John continued to feel guilty about having abandoned Julian and Cynthia, he'd be damned if he was going to be like every other rich asshole father who'd abandoned his family and then used money as a poor substitute for love and companionship. He was simply not going to give Julian money every time he asked for it. Julian was too young and irresponsible. Anyway, he was well taken care of. He wasn't going hungry. He didn't need more money. What was he going to do with it? Buy more beer? Let him earn some bloody money on his own. Learn the value of a *quid*. Maybe when he turned 21 he'd give him a bit more money, but definitely not before that.

BORN AGAIN

JOHN AND YOKO WERE IN THE EL SALANO DEN WATCHING the Grammy awards on television when Bob Dylan, a.k.a. Robert Zimmerman, a Jew turned born-again Christian, sang his latest hit, *Serve Someone*. The song's message: It doesn't matter who you are or what you do, you're going to have to serve either Satan or God.

Hearing it for the first time drove John off his rocker. He thought about how, three years earlier, in a moment of weakness, he, too, had embraced Jesus Christ. Granted, it was only a brief flirtation, lasting about two weeks. But for a man who had once claimed that the Beatles were "more popular than Jesus" and had nearly gotten himself crucified for saying it, it was a radical departure.

John, in 1977, out of sheer boredom, had taken to watching preachers on TV. It was something else to do besides sleep and program dreams. Despite his better judgment, he somehow became a big fan of the Reverend Billy Graham. At first he watched only for entertainment. Then, one day, he had an epiphany—he allowed himself to be touched by the love of Jesus Christ, and it drove him to tears of joy and ecstasy. He drew a picture of a crucifix; he was *born again*, and the experience was such a kick, he had to share it with Yoko.

John and Yoko sat in front of the TV watching Billy Graham sermons. Every other sentence out of John's mouth was *Thank You, Jesus* or *Thank You, Lord*. Then, as quickly as Jesus came, Jesus went, and John apologized to Yoko for subjecting her to Billy Graham.

Now here was Bob Dylan shilling for Jesus at the Grammys and it was more than John could bear. He used to respect Dylan—they were almost friends. He was also strongly influenced by him. *I Am the Walrus* was a prime example of his Dylanesque phase; John used oblique phrases in that song to give the impression that he was saying more than he really was. "A good game," he called it. But in 1970, just after leaving the Beatles, he formally renounced Dylan *and* Jesus, singing on *God,* which appeared on *Plastic Ono Band,* his first solo album, that he didn't believe in either one. Pointedly, in this song he called Dylan by his real name, Zimmerman.

Now everything John had grown to despise was in *Serve Someone.* He felt so much rage and disgust that he picked up his guitar and began strumming and singing. The result was *Serve Yourself,* a wrathful protest song bristling with fury and despair—raw, primal Lennon lashing out at everything and everybody: Jesus, Buddha, Mohammed, Krishna, his sons, his mother...the world.

Lennon's musical howl can be paraphrased like this: *Nobody's gonna do shit for you, kid, so you better fucking do it for yourself. And speaking of fucking kids—I'm talkin' to you young Jude—Bah! You're just like all the others. You think I'm gonna buy you a fucking Mercedes Benz. Go to bloody hell and praise the fucking lord for the fucking shirt on your fucking back!*

Then he stopped playing the guitar and cried out for mother...any mother. *It's mother who's responsible for everything 'cause she brought you into this bloody, shit-stained world.*

Four months later he'd record the song, but this primal version would only be released 19 years later, on *The John Lennon Anthology.*

GOING BACK TO NEW YORK CITY

THE CREATION OF MORE MUSIC WOULD HAVE TO WAIT. Mercury Retrograde was closing in, and it was imperative that the Lennons get back to New York City immediately. Yoko, again in the fetal position, sat in a club chair in the El Salano entrance hall. Surrounded by her new $17,000 birthday wardrobe, she supervised the gofers as they scurried to and fro, packing clothing, lugging trunks, confirming and reconfirming reservations.

John and Yoko always demanded that the servants treat their possessions with care and respect. But the road show was not proceeding smoothly. John was screaming at the gofers because he thought they were carrying the trunks carelessly. To make his point, he carried an enormous suitcase out to the limousine, strained his back and blamed it on the servants. Then, as if Mercury Retrograde had already begun, the airline reservations got fouled up. When they arrived at the airport, they were told that no first class seats were available. They had to fly coach on Eastern Airlines. It was the kind of situation John dreaded. The other passengers gawked at him, demanded his autograph. There was no escape. John sat by the window, wearing dark glasses, feigning sleep. Yoko and Sean, wrapped in a blanket, were curled up next to him.

CANNON HILL

OWN & COUNTRY MAGAZINE ARRIVED IN THE MAIL, addressed to Dr. Winston O'Boogie. John immediately turned to the back page and examined Patric Walker's horoscope, first Libra for him, then Aquarius for Yoko.

> *Libra: This March your mood will change from elation to dejection and back. You will want to spend much more time on your own which may cause problems with partners. However, before you begin to imagine that it's the life of a hermit for you now, it must be said that periods such as these are frequently extremely productive. Fortunately for you the financial picture is unusually bright, and even when you do feel you are suffering, it ought to be in relative comfort.*
>
> *Aquarius: You must decide this month what you are striving for and how much you're prepared to sacrifice to achieve it. You must seek greater financial security and stability. March promises to be an outstanding month for not only your professional interests, but also your personal prestige.*

After quietly waiting out Mercury Retrograde at the Dakota, the Lennons and their entourage ventured out on March 21, 1980, the first day of spring, to their country retreat in Cold Spring Harbor, Long Island.

It was the first time they'd been to Cannon Hill since late November, right after they had bought the estate. Then, the mansion was virtually empty, save for the decaying furniture the previous owners had left behind. Yoko, wanting to baptize the place with a real American Thanksgiving, invited her nephew to join them. John loved being surrounded by family.

Uda-San cooked the turkey while Penny King, an excellent chef and the overseer of the Lennons' upstate New York farm property (where Yoko kept her cows), prepared an organic baked lasagna and a half-dozen apple and pecan pies.

John was delighted to meet King for the first time.

Dressed for dinner in a T-shirt, his hair tied back samurai-style, he made a grand display of carving the big bird. It was the perfect family Thanksgiving except for one problem: the house was infested with fleas. Everybody got them, and the Lennons and their servants fled Cannon Hill scratching.

By March 1980, for their second visit, Cannon Hill had been thoroughly fumigated and exquisitely renovated by Sam Havadtoy, the interior decorator who would become Yoko's live-in boyfriend after John's death.

The spring weather was gorgeous and John sat in the backyard all afternoon, looking out at Long Island Sound, entranced by the boats sailing by. Yoko, wearing a sweat suit, ran around on the grass and wrestled with Sean. John snapped Polaroids. Sean ran over to examine each one as it developed. A servant took pictures of John taking pictures of Sean and Yoko. A video camera on a tripod, filming everybody taking pictures of everybody else, was left running the entire time. This tape—eerie, heartbreaking footage of John, Yoko and Sean looking out at the water—would be used nine months later in Yoko's *Thin Ice* video.

One afternoon Sean saw two birds mating. He ran to the house to tell John about it—in detail. John took the opportunity to explain the facts of life to Sean. You make babies by putting your "pee-pee" in the woman, he told him. "Everybody does it."

"I know," Sean replied. "I once saw two crabs do it on the beach. How would a crab and a bird do it?"

John explained that everybody sticks with their own species.

Later, Sean went fishing and caught five flounder. Ever the proud daddy, John took a Polaroid of Sean and his fish, and that night Uda-San cooked the fish for dinner.

Another afternoon, while John napped, Sean and Yoko sat in the backyard discussing God.

"God is everywhere," Sean speculated. "God is a doo-doo."

A PLAN

BY NOW, A NUMBER OF THINGS HAD CLARIFIED THEMSELVES in John's head. The only way to emerge from five years of silence and seclusion, he knew, was to release an LP. It would be an album of family songs, half his, half Yoko's. From this point on, he was determined to make Yoko an equal partner in all his creative ventures.

He'd decided, too, that he was going to fulfill another long-standing ambition—he was going to sail to Bermuda. That was where he'd write the music for this new album. According to Yoko's calculations, Bermuda was in the right direction, and Swan's cards were in agreement—it was the *only* place to go. John toyed with, though ultimately rejected, the idea of breaking the ice for the album by releasing an EP titled *Bermuda Shorts.*

John had first become interested in sailing in 1975. As Yoko's pregnancy with Sean entered the final difficult months, he relieved his tension by going with friends, such as Richard Ross, on sailing trips to Martha's Vineyard and Long Island. He loved it; it was great exercise. He thought that with practice and discipline he'd eventually be able to sail a boat as well as he played the guitar. Sailing, John sensed, was closely related to music. To create music he had to be centered, and what better way to get centered than on an ocean voyage to Bermuda. It would be exactly what he needed to get back on The Path and achieve the pure lifestyle of Jesus or Gandhi, men who were the antithesis of everything he'd become— the ultimate consumer forever in search of instant gratification. Instant gratification had been too easy for too many years, and he feared that his power to have anything he wanted when he wanted it had corrupted him totally.

At sea, John knew, you must always concentrate, be perpetually vigilant and alert. There was a danger of being overrun by ships or commandeered by pirates. By putting himself in a potentially dangerous situation, his material cravings would disappear. He'd be forced to achieve a higher level of consciousness.

John spent his days studying sailing books, magazines, and ocean charts. To learn how to sail, he bought a 14-foot sailboat and named it Isis after the Egyptian goddess of fertility. Then he hired as his sailing instructor Tyler Coneys, the young man who ran the boat dealership where he bought the Isis. Sailing lessons began immediately. As John and his mentor cruised around Long Island Sound, he knew he was doing the right thing.

"Yabba dabba doo!" he'd cry when he caught a full sail of wind. Then he'd call out to his rock 'n' roll neighbor who also owned a home on Long Island's Gold Coast: "Where are you, Billy Joel? I love your album!" He was talking about Joel's classic LP *Glass Houses*, which had been released that year.

As John's confidence grew, he took Sean sailing with him. He wanted Sean to learn the traditional English survival skills: sailing, swimming, lifesaving, boxing. He'd already begun giving him swimming lessons at the YMCA. Should he ever be thrust into the outside world, Sean had to be able to take care of himself.

One time the Isis capsized, but he and Tyler were easily able to right the boat. It was no big deal, and John was undaunted. He was making progress daily, and Tyler was an excellent teacher. John appreciated the sailing lessons so much that he once invited Tyler to share a joint with him. Tyler considered John his friend, and he was already searching for the proper ship to charter for Lennon's intended Bermuda voyage. He had told his cousins to stand by. If this voyage really came to pass, they were going to be John Lennon's crew.

But before they set sail there were certain things, both spiritual and carnal, that John needed to accomplish.

VOW OF SILENCE

T THE END OF MARCH, JOHN TOOK A VOW OF
silence, a vital step on the road to being centered. It had
been years since he'd attempted anything like this, and he knew
how long and difficult the journey would be. He prayed to God for
the willpower and conviction to continue to lead a pure life once the
vow ended. If he was going to succeed, he'd have to accept himself
as a deeply flawed human being, and follow in the footsteps of
Gandhi with grace and humility. John knew that everything he
wanted was there, in Cannon Hill. All else did not exist.

For ten days John remained in total silence, meditating frequently. All was calm, all was still.

He tried not to communicate with anyone. Occasionally, he
gesticulated or wrote notes, but he felt that was cheating.

"Silence is golden," one note said.

He kept to a strict diet of herbal tea, nuts, raisins, yogurt, salt-free
bread, and sour herbs. Not drinking coffee was the most difficult part;
he went through caffeine withdrawal, which, as usual, was agony.

He filled his time drawing, making collages, and studying boat
brochures, books and ocean charts. Magazines, newspapers and fic-
tion were not allowed, Yoko said.

He went sailing alone.

His silence drove the servants crazy. They didn't understand
what he was doing, or why. John still expected them to anticipate
his every wish and be totally supportive. But they laughed at him
behind his back. Once he overheard two servants sitting in the
kitchen cracking jokes about him. Furious, he barged in, smashed a
tea cup in the sink, and ran out.

Yoko witnessed the silent vow in awe, mesmerized by his
willpower and discipline. "The man is so powerful," she said. This
was the John she loved.

When the ten days of silence ended, John shaved his beard, the last beard he would ever grow, the one he'd begun just before Thanksgiving 1979.

To be beardless felt good.

Then he sat in a club chair in the living room smoking a pipe.

CAPE TOWN

Libra: You may be quite prepared to make a complete break from the past now and set up shop in a totally new environment. The stage is set for a new saga and throughout the remainder of 1980 you will be striving for greater freedom as well as recognition. Mercury eclipsed by the Moon on Sunday the 13th in Pisces makes you almost clairvoyant about your future role in life.

Aquarius: You are going to be hard-put to remain totally buoyant and optimistic this April. Relatives are likely to drive you to distraction. You don't need an astrologer to tell you that 1980 so far has been a precarious year. You may have to stand your ground, even if it means telling the truth and shaming the devil.

THE LAST WEEK OF APRIL 1980, YOKO TOLD JOHN THAT a karmically cleansing directional voyage to the south and east was imperative—he was to leave immediately for Cape Town, South Africa. This was, perhaps, a peculiar choice of destination. The South African Broadcasting Company had banned Beatles music for five years in the wake of John's 1966 comment that the group was more popular than Jesus. And even after lifting the ban, they kept Lennon's solo work blacklisted. Nonetheless, he jumped at the opportunity to get away. Even though he thought the karmic cleansing was a load of bloody crap, he felt the isolation would be beneficial. And having been to C-town before, he knew that it was a good place to get jacked off.

The journey inspired John. He took notes on everything: the scenery, the cab ride to Cape Town from the airport, and his cab driver and self-appointed tour guide, Mohammed.

After checking into the Mount Nelson Hotel under an assumed

name, John went shopping for a raincoat, shampoo and macrobiotic fruit.

Back at the hotel bar, he couldn't figure out how much money to put in the cigarette machine. A businessman who recognized him from the plane offered him a cigarette, which he happily accepted.

That day, every time John set foot outside his hotel room, somebody recognized him. Strangers offered him drugs and whores, but he declined. A pretty, blonde hotel waitress tried to pick him up, but he turned her down. The last thing he wanted was a story in the gossip rags about being seen in public with a waitress.

Alone in his room, he clipped classified ads for massage parlors from a local sex tabloid.

The next day, in a massage parlor, John got jerked off. But it was disappointing. The woman was doing her job—nothing more. She wasn't into it at all. He dropped his trousers, she squirted some lotion on his cock, then stroke...stroke...spurt. It was over fast and he was out of there.

John sat in his hotel room that night reading the local newspaper. An article reported that he'd been spotted buying a raincoat. He felt strange—like a flying saucer.

He suspected reporters had somehow gotten into his hotel room while he was out.

Later in the week, he telephoned May Pang. She was depressed and unemployed. They chatted for an hour; he promised to send her a postcard. Next he telephoned Yoko. She played a tape of a song she'd just written. John thought that the lyrics were great, but he was concerned that the muse had given Yoko exactly one melody, which she was doomed to repeat for the rest of her life. He asked God to inspire his wife.

The following afternoon, John sat in his hotel room eating his macrobiotic fruit. He decided to return to the massage parlor.

This time it was much better. He hooked up with Louise, a large-breasted blonde. She was really into getting him excited. First she gave him a little tit-show, peeling off her blouse, her boobs springing forth from her front-opening bra. Then she was naked and so was John. She squirted lots of baby oil on her hands, and sensuously massaged it into his cock. Then, for effect, she rubbed the oil all over her breasts, until they gleamed.

"You like my tits?" she said, pressing them against him.

With one hand she tickled his balls. With the other she stroked his cock, slowly, slowly. "Come on, shoot it all over me."

And shoot off he did, like fucking Portnoy.

Yes, John thought, this was the hand job of his dreams, slow, sensual nostalgia, just like when he was a teenager.

The next day John returned to Cold Spring Harbor, only the tarot card reader Charlie Swan aware of exactly what he'd been doing in Africa. It was now May and the Libran stars were looking very good, indeed:

With your ruler, Venus, twinkling away at the midheaven of your solar horoscope you have got to be on the threshold of a new and exciting chapter in your career.

VOYAGE TO BERMUDA

Libra: You should be enjoying foreign travel at this time since there is so much planetary activity in the sign of Gemini and the foreign angle of your personal chart. Don't be surprised if the entire pattern of your present life is changed in a very short time. It could be called a turning point of your life, and since Pluto in your birth sign is magnificently aspected by the Sun on June 9, you can look forward with high hopes to achieving success in a totally new setting.

Aquarius: You should be extremely happy and even deeply involved in a new love affair this month because the Sun and Venus are passing through your angle of good fortune and romance.

IN EARLY JUNE, AFTER ANOTHER MONTH OF INTENSIVE sailing lessons, it was time to leave for Bermuda. John and his crew, Tyler Coneys and his cousins, Kevin and Ellen Coneys, gathered for breakfast at Cannon Hill, then left for the airport, accompanied by Sean.

As John boarded the small plane, Sean pleaded with him to be careful. He was terrified that his daddy would be hurt.

John missed Sean already.

They flew to Newport, Rhode Island, where they met Captain Hank, owner of the Megan Jaye, the schooner that Tyler Coneys had chartered for the trip. The band of five, which now included Captain Hank, set sail. For the first two days, with strong, steady winds and a calm sea, the sailing was excellent. Then, on the third day, a violent storm struck; everybody but John and Captain Hank were incapacitated by seasickness. Hank stood at the helm until he was too exhausted to keep his eyes open.

"Do you want to take the wheel?" he finally asked John.

"If it's okay by you, it's okay by me."

"It's okay by me."

"Just keep an eye on me," John said, taking the helm.

Captain Hank watched him steer for about fifteen minutes. Satisfied that John knew what he was doing, he went below to the cabin. Time passed, and it dawned on John that Hank had no intention of returning until he'd slept for a few hours. It was up to him now; four lives were in his hands. At first he was afraid. But his confidence slowly grew. He *did* know what he was doing. Then he realized that for the first time in years he was actually having fun.

Wearing an Arab headdress and yellow slicker, John stayed at the helm of the Megan Jaye as 40-mph winds and huge waves battered the ship. He was proud of himself. The crew had turned green and passed out around him. The professional sailors couldn't hack the heavy weather. The househusband was in command. Fear and tension occasionally drove him to the verge of panic, but he fought it off. He screamed into the wind and sang Irish sea chanteys like a crazed Viking.

John manned the helm for five straight hours, keeping the Megan Jaye on course.

Still the bad weather continued, and still the Coneyses continued to vomit up their guts, but John didn't get seasick. His father was a sailor, and maybe the ocean was in his blood. Eventually Captain Hank retook the wheel and John went below to boil water for tea. Later he made coffee and cooked brown rice, which he ate with chopsticks. He was famished.

On the fourth day the radio antenna broke and Captain Hank had to navigate like Magellan, using only a sextant and the location of the sun and the stars.

John continually dreamed of Sean. He looked upon these dreams as bad omens and feared that something had happened. But with the radio out, there was no way to get in touch with anyone, and he had to contain his panic. Visions of Yoko's spirit comforted him.

On the seventh day, after a voyage of a thousand miles, John, feeling centered, piloted the good ship Megan Jaye into St. George Harbor, Bermuda.

KNAPTON HILL

As soon as John landed in Bermuda, he called Yoko to tell her of his dreams about Sean. She assured him that Sean was fine, and that she'd send him down in a day or two. John asked Yoko when she was coming to Bermuda. "I miss you," he said. She told him she wasn't coming. She had a head cold and needed to rest. Besides, according to the O, this was not a good time for her to travel. The news saddened John, but there was nothing he could do to change it.

John and the Coneys clan moved into House Alexandria, a small cottage on Knapton Hill, about five miles outside Hamilton, the main city. John spent the day washing his clothes, the first time he'd done laundry in longer than he could remember. But doing it felt good. That night, everybody celebrated their safe arrival with a home-cooked feast.

With John in the master bedroom and the Coneyses camped out all over the living room, the cottage was crowded. When Sean and three servants arrived the following day, it became wall-to-wall people. John couldn't stand it. He was getting claustrophobic and panicky. He'd had no privacy in over a week. The Coneys family, with nothing to distract them, couldn't help staring at him. Every night he called Yoko, but she still had a cold. The tarot readings hadn't improved, either. And business required her undivided attention. She flatly refused to come to Bermuda.

VILLA
UNDERCLIFFE

AN ASSISTANT, DISPATCHED TO SCOUT THE ISLAND FOR A larger, more appropriate house, found Villa Undercliffe in a matter of hours. Totally secluded, the gothic, 350-year-old mansion was located at the end of an unmarked dirt road in Fairylands, an exclusive waterfront community just outside Hamilton. Here John could have both the privacy to create and the convenience of being only minutes from the city, should he need to recharge himself with a spontaneous shopping spree. There was also a huge backyard for Sean to play in, and a small dock where John could sit and look out at the harbor or launch the Sunfish, a tiny sailboat. It was perfect and John loved it.

There was one minor problem. The owners, Rolf and Molly Luthi, who had two teenage children, didn't want to rent it out immediately. But when told who the prospective tenant was, and that he was willing to pay $24,000 for six weeks, they agreed to vacate. The Luthis were on their way out as the Lennon entourage —minus the Coneys clan, who had been ditched at House Alexandria now that they were no longer needed—was on its way in.

Workmen were doing repairs; they had no idea who the new tenants were.

"My dad's a Beatle," Sean told a plumber.

"Mine's a cockroach," the plumber replied.

Exhausted, tense, and very pale, John settled into the master bedroom on the second floor of Villa Undercliffe. From the antique four-post bed, where he'd spend many hours gazing out the window at the tiny islands dotting Hamilton Harbor, the view was spectacular. At sunset, the world looked like paradise. But without Yoko, in these unfamiliar surroundings—the stranger's room that John would eventually sing about in *I'm Losing You*—he'd sometimes feel disoriented and purposeless. He had yet to embrace the muse. The music had not yet begun to flow. And it wouldn't flow for weeks.

AMERICAN TOURIST

THOUGH JOHN HAD COME TO BERMUDA TO WRITE MUSIC and record a demo tape, *Double Fantasy* remained only a germ of an idea. He had not yet achieved the correct creative frame of mind. He needed more time. And before going to work he also wanted to have some fun, check out the island, explore those pink sand beaches. Unfortunately, that could be dangerous. It was one thing to be occasionally recognized in the street. But he did not want it publicly known that he was going to be staying in Bermuda at least through July. It's a tiny island with no place to hide. If he was going to create new music, a modicum of privacy was imperative.

Declaring himself a phantom, John did his chameleon act. One day he'd disguise himself with a pair of sunglasses and a Panama hat pulled way down over his eyes. The next day he'd wear a khaki safari outfit, his hair tied back in a ponytail. For two weeks John, Sean and their entourage of servants explored Bermuda on foot, on bicycle and by chauffeur-driven car. At first, nobody recognized him...just another rich American tourist on holiday with the kid and the servants.

On the Queen's birthday John took Sean to Hamilton Harbor to watch the parade. There was a 21-gun salute, and the governor marched around in a big, white, feathered hat. In the middle of the massive crowd, John and Sean stood unnoticed.

That evening, at the dinner table, Sean began acting up—playing with his food, eating with his hands instead of a fork.

"Eat properly, as you've been taught," John scolded him, an edge in his voice.

Sean threw a forkful of mashed potatoes at John. John ignored it. Sean grabbed a pair of chopsticks and stuck them in his nose. "I'm the walrus," he said.

"You're not like other children!" John screamed. "Mommy and I are going to be taking you all over the world. We're going to be eating with kings and queens. You've got to listen to me when I teach you about table manners. Otherwise you won't be able to come with us!"

Sean began to sulk, and John sent him to his room, warning him not to come out till he was ready to apologize.

When Sean emerged from his room a half hour later, John was sitting on the dock behind the house. "I'm sorry," Sean said tearfully.

John kissed him, and Sean went back to the house. He seemed distant, though, John thought, and he began to fear that Sean was angry with him, that he was losing him, that they'd never be close again. Then he tried calling Yoko in New York but couldn't get through. He spent the evening in a state of acute anxiety, convinced that he was losing everybody he loved.

The next afternoon John asked Sean if he wanted to go out for a snack. Delighted, Sean agreed, and the chauffeur drove them to Front Street, Hamilton's main drag. John bought Sean a hot chocolate and donut at a cafe. Sean was thrilled that Daddy was buying him forbidden foods. John was thrilled that they were friends again, growing close again. Even if it meant feeding him sugar, it was worth it.

A man sitting at a nearby table spotted John and walked over. "Your music meant a lot to me," he said, asking for an autograph.

Graciously scribbling his name on a napkin, John decided it was a perfect afternoon. When he got back to Villa Undercliffe, he praised the Lord: *Thank You. Thank You. Thank You.* Sometimes he still needed to be recognized by strangers.

John and Sean continued to get along well. They went bike riding the next day and got drenched in a downpour. The following afternoon he took Sean to the Warwick Riding Academy. Having never done any serious horseback riding, John suddenly got the urge to give it a go and registered as Mr. Winston. His hair was tied back in a ponytail, and he was wearing his Panama hat. People stared at him but couldn't seem to place the face—not even the riding instructor, a young woman from Liverpool whose mother had seen the Beatles perform at The Cavern. She took John and his entourage along a narrow, rocky trail. On one side was a sheer cliff. Scared out of his wits, John was convinced he was going to fall to his death. Then it began to rain again. The group turned back. By the time John and Sean got home, they were soaked to the skin.

Mostly, John and his cortege ducked into pubs and restaurants on Front Street. Sometimes they were recognized. John enjoyed signing the occasional autograph and listening to people praise his music. But in one restaurant a teenage girl followed him into the bathroom.

"Are you who I think you are?" she asked, bug-eyed, as John peed in a urinal.

"Who do you think I am?" he replied, zipping his fly, barging past her.

At night John lay in bed listening to the BBC World News Service on the radio. It made him homesick for England, but not enough to want to return. If he ever went back, it was going to be as the conquering hero. He was going to cruise up the Thames on a ship, like Eric the Red.

Some afternoons he spent on the porch behind the house, meditating in the sunshine, working on his tan. Occasionally he went swimming or took the Sunfish for a spin around the harbor. Mostly, though, he thought about how much he missed Yoko.

Each night, as the sun went down, somewhere on the other side of the harbor somebody played bagpipes. The music drifted across the water, and John listened, enchanted by it. He wondered who the musician was, considered searching for him, playing music together. But he never did.

One afternoon John took Sean to the Botanical Gardens. Everything was in bloom; it was beautiful. The gardens were meticulously kept, every plant labeled. They walked hand-in-hand, John pointing out the plants to Sean, reading the names: *Angel Wings*, *Purple Imperator*, *White Excelsior*. Then they came upon a flower from the freesia family. Double Fantasy, it was called. John, studying the sign closely, said the name out loud, and delighted by the sound, he said it again. It was a good name...an excellent name.

At night John sat in the living room with Sean and the servants watching *WKRP in Cincinnati* on TV. He thought he should be doing something else. But he liked looking at Loni Anderson; "eye candy," he called her. And what else was there to do? Go to a disco? Sit at the bar and listen to music he couldn't stand while strangers demanded autographs? That scene had already played itself out for him by 1965. Too many nights and too many scotches and cokes at London's Ad Lib and Bag O' Nails and Scotch of St. James, talking to Mick Jagger till dawn about music and who was the greatest rock 'n' roll band in the world.

The only music he listened to these days was soft classical or Muzak on the radio, and even that was dangerous, 'cause he never knew when they'd play a song by fucking McCartney. If he wanted to go to discos, he could go to Studio 54 in New York...be seen with Andy Warhol...be written up in the gossip columns. *Fuck Andy Warhol! He was a bloody wanker when I was conquering the fucking world!* He was not about to start frequenting Bermudian discos.

So he remained a homebody, going to sleep early and rising at dawn. If he was going to create music, and it was imperative that he start doing it soon, this was the kind of routine he had to maintain. The fact that he'd done absolutely nothing worthwhile since he'd arrived in Bermuda was beginning to gnaw at him.

Every day he did the Front Street shopping and café routine. He was being seen too much, and sometimes it embarrassed him that he still had the need to be recognized. It was better to be a phantom like he was in New York. He understood that much of his mystique and power came from his inaccessibility. Fans had not yet come knocking at the door of Villa Undercliffe, seeking autographs and knowledge. But if he kept it up, it was only a matter of time. The house may have been secluded, but once people found out where it was, it was vulnerable, and only a fifteen-minute walk from downtown Hamilton. If a "troupie" scene developed in Fairylands, that would pretty much insure that the music would never be written.

NIGHT LIFE

ONE NIGHT, WHEN IT WAS TOO QUIET IN THE HOUSE, when there was nothing on TV and he didn't feel like going to sleep, John was overcome by a sudden urge to go to a disco. Perhaps it would be fun after all, he thought. He was supposed to be making a record album and there wouldn't be any harm in checking out what the kids were listening to these days, would there?

Accompanied by his personal assistant Fred Seaman, John ventured into Flavors on Front Street. It reminded him of the clubs in Hamburg twenty years earlier. Nothing had changed but the music; now they were playing disco.

He wanted to get high. Handing Seaman a hundred-dollar bill, he told him to score cocaine. It was difficult to come by any kind of drug in Bermuda; customs were tight, the laws tough, and the soil was not good for growing marijuana. But motivated by John's sudden craving—and the fact that he'd already been snagged at customs with a quaalude but was let go 'cause he worked for John Lennon and John Lennon was good for Bermuda's economy—Seaman hit up a black dude in the bathroom who was selling some kind of white powder that he claimed was coke.

"Let's do it," John said when Seaman returned.

They snorted it in a toilet stall. The "coke" was mostly speed. *Figures.*

A *Royal Gazette* reporter spotted him and demanded an interview.

"I don't do interviews," John replied.

The reporter threatened to write a negative story.

"Fuck off," John told him. "I expect as much. Nobody ever writes the truth about me anyway."

No such story appeared.

John was leaning against the bar sipping an English beer when he became aware of the music. The B-52s' *Rock Lobster* was blasting over the sound system, and one of the women in the band sounded exactly like Yoko yowling. He'd never heard it before and was astonished.

"Who are they?" he asked Seaman.

Seaman told him.

"Get out the ax and call Mother!" John cried. "They're ready for us at last!"

John woke up the next morning sick as a dog, hungover from his glass of beer. But there was no need to go back to the disco for further research. He'd seen and heard enough.

BIRTH
OF A SONG

URING HIS YEARS OF SECLUSION, JOHN COMPOSED dozens of songs, including *Popcorn* and a tribute to playwright Tennessee Williams titled *Tennessee*. He even wrote a song about David Bowie. But he never released any of this material because he thought it was mediocre, paint-by-numbers bullshit. If he had released it, he'd have been no better than McCartney at his worst.

Since the day Sean was born, John knew he wanted to do an album about family, domestic bliss. The idea had been buzzing around in his brain for five years; every few months another tiny piece of the puzzle came to him. Long before he came up with the *Double Fantasy* concept, he wrote *Dream Family*, a clichéd *Double Fantasy*-style song.

In the autumn of 1978, John had dinner with a business associate, Norman Seaman. Seaman, the husband of Sean's nanny, Helen, and the uncle of John's personal assistant, Fred, was a minor league impresario who in the early 1960's had produced Yoko's performance art pieces at Carnegie Recital Hall. Unable to understand why John wasn't doing everything in his power to make as much money as possible, Seaman questioned the ex-Beatle's sanity. He told him that if he didn't come out of hiding immediately, people would forget him, and he'd never be able to get his career back on track.

John knew that Seaman wasn't the only one who thought he was out of his mind. Everybody had always thought so. People called him *Crazy John*. This was the title of a song Tom Paxton had written about him. But it wasn't until John was in Bermuda, two years after Norman Seaman had questioned his sanity, that he composed his own song about people thinking he was crazy, *Watching the Wheels*. As soon as he wrote the song, he knew it was something major and he praised the Lord for his inspiration.

The Buddy Holly–like line from *Beautiful Boy*, about things getting better every day, popped into John's head in April 1979, when Julian was with him in Palm Beach. It was the first time he ever saw Sean and Julian playing together, and it filled him with hope that someday his entire family would be reunited.

Then, in Bermuda, for the first time in years, John was able to let go of his fear and boredom and misery. Instead, he concentrated on the ecstatic moments of perfection: the times that he and Yoko could still be friends and spend hours together smoking and talking, just like the old days; the sex that was once extraordinary; and those remarkable days when he got along with Sean and it seemed as if God had granted him everything he'd ever wanted—the love of a family. It was corny and simple and beautiful and painful. The idea that familial bliss could be achieved, had been achieved, yet was always so brief and elusive, as if the whole world conspired to prevent it—this is what he'd communicate in *Double Fantasy*. But it wouldn't be easy.

By late June 1980, John had still not completed one song that would make it on to the LP. While the shock of hearing the B-52's imitating Yoko was enough to get him to sit down with his guitar, it took Paul McCartney to give John the final push he needed to get on track.

Though thinking of Paul caused John pain, he could never get McCartney out of his head; Paul's music was everywhere, and it always made him jealous, even the songs he enjoyed.

In Bermuda, John was listening to all kinds of things on the radio, not just the Muzak and classical he listened to in New York. *Coming Up*, Paul's hit single from *McCartney II*, was unavoidable. Every time he tuned in the BBC or one of the local stations, there it was. It began to drive John crackers. Paul was calling for a Beatles reunion, and every word of the song was addressed directly to him. Ultimately, he came to admire it and draw inspiration from it.

The small room next door to the master bedroom had been converted to a two-track recording studio complete with rhythm box. To get into gear for the demo tape, John played *Coming Up* on his guitar over and over, sometimes improvising his own words, sometimes singing Paul's words, which spoke of peace and the possibility of again playing music together.

Paul's lyrics forced John to at last write a complete song. Though *I Don't Wanna Face It* would not make it on to *Double Fantasy*, it would be included on the posthumous sequel, *Milk and Honey*, transformed into a primal rocker sounding something like a cut from *Plastic Ono Band*. Communicating his despair and loss of identity, John, playing off Paul's words from *Coming Up*, sings of himself in the second person, admitting that he wants to save the world, but doesn't know how he can when at heart he's really just a hard-core misanthrope.

Then as the song fades out, John cries, "Every time I look in the mirror I don't see anybody there!"

The next song John wrote, *Borrowed Time*, was a prophetic, haunting statement set to a reggae beat. He simply acknowledges the doom he's felt in his soul for decades. Death may be close by, he says, but that's okay. Death is release. Life is a burden. He's done it all and there's nothing left to do.

This, too, would be released posthumously on *Milk and Honey*.

Even though these songs were not what he had in mind for *Double Fantasy*, for the moment it didn't matter. He was creating inspired material and felt ecstatic about it. After recording each song, he thanked God for the inspiration. Then he called Yoko in New York and played the tape for her over the telephone. Yoko would in turn play for John the songs she'd been recording. Their mutual misery had been transformed into mutual inspiration. They were communicating with music, feeding off each other's energy.

Yet, when he pleaded with Yoko to please come to Bermuda, she said she still had a cold and was feeling weak. John pointed out that she'd had a cold for two months, and the problem was that she didn't eat right—*too much junk food and chocolate and crap like that*. Yoko disagreed. The reason she was sick was because John was mean to her and she needed more love.

Hanging up the phone, John retreated to the Villa Undercliffe studio and finished off *Dear Yoko*. There's one notable difference between the demo tape and the version that appears on *Double Fantasy*. On the LP, the last line says that the goddess smiled upon their love. On the demo the goddess frowned.

MOTHER'S ARRIVAL

ON JUNE 27, WITH MERCURY RETROGRADE ONLY TWO DAYS away, Yoko, against her better judgment, agreed to come to Bermuda. John was thrilled. "Mommy's coming today," he told Sean.

But John's assistant arrived at the airport too late to meet Yoko's flight, and he found her wandering in a daze, muttering "Nobody loves me."

Mother's mood was foul when she got to Villa Undercliffe. John tried to cheer her up by performing his completed version of *Serve Yourself*, the anthem he'd written in Palm Beach as a response to Dylan.

Despite her mood, Yoko was stunned by the song's raw power and cried, "That's it!"

The next day, in yet another futile attempt to make Mother happy, John took Yoko on a Front Street shopping spree. John's favorite store, The English Sport Shop, reminded him of the places he'd frequented in London in the 1960's; he felt at home there. Leaving Yoko to browse downstairs in the Scottish plaid department, John went upstairs to be custom-fitted for a conservative wool suit.

"I want something a banker would wear," he told the manager, who suggested a fine cut of gray flannel, which John liked.

The manager measured John and asked him how he wanted to pay for the suit.

John gave him his New York address and told him to bill it to "Jack Green."

"Is that your usual alias, Mr. Lennon?" the manager asked.

John laughed.

The manager, who was originally from Sheffield, England,

about 60 miles east of Liverpool, admitted that he was a Beatles fan. John told him about a hotel in Sheffield where the Beatles had stayed in 1962.

"I know it well," the manager said. "A dreadful place."

"Yes," John agreed.

Meanwhile, down in the women's department, Yoko was buying everything in sight.

John returned to the English Sport Shop the next day to pick up some shirts and accessories to go with the suit. He dropped an additional two thousand dollars. The manager had his copy of *Mind Games* on hand. John autographed it. The suit would be made in England and shipped to New York via Bermuda. It would arrive in November. John would like the suit very much and wear it exactly once.

Saturday night, to beat the onset of Mercury Retrograde, Yoko, still in a miserable mood, flew back to New York. John was so relieved when she left that he wrote *I'm Stepping Out*, a paean to his desire to get away from Mother. It was not her favorite song, and it, too, would not be released until *Milk and Honey*.

Later that week, a wire service article appeared in the local paper, *The Royal Gazette*, announcing that Yoko had sold one of her prize Holstein cows at the New York State fair in Syracuse for a record-shattering $265,000. Declaring another great victory over the McCartneys, John clipped the article and called Yoko to congratulate her.

The Holstein incident would inevitably be immortalized on *Double Fantasy*. "Don't sell a cow!" John cries out at the end of *Dear Yoko*. "Spend some time with me and Sean!"

Nonetheless, John celebrated Yoko's business acumen by taking Sean to a nearby dairy farm to watch the cows being milked. Sean had a great time, and John did, too. It reminded him of Liverpool, when he was six years old, living in Mendips with his Aunt Mimi and Uncle George, who ran a dairy farm around the corner. Sometimes in the morning, George would take him to watch the cows being milked.

And suddenly John noticed he was missing Mother very badly.

INSPIRATION

Libra: Mars enters your own birth sign this July and acts as the catalyst which throughout the remainder of 1980 transforms your life. It is important that you have a clearer idea of what your next career move should be. But because Mercury will be in Retrograde motion at the very zenith of your solar chart until July 23, you may be inclined to put off making a final commitment. Don't, for now is the time to strengthen and enhance your position. Personally and emotionally the coming months will be exciting and memorable, but you must understand that Saturn follows Mars into Libra in late September and this time the foundation you lay down will be your own Rock of Gibraltar.

Aquarius: There are very few adverse planetary aspects this month and were it not for the fact that Mercury is in retrograde motion until the 23rd in your angle of general work and career interests, you could be blazing quite a number of new trails. The magnificent aspects of your ruling planet Uranus this July can give you star billing. Developments around the 8th or 13th of the month will make even some of your wildest dreams a reality.

O N JUNE 29, WHEN MERCURY RETROGRADE SET IN AGAIN, it hit John hard. Cut off from Mother, he felt adrift, frightened, insecure. Everything was going wrong. Why did Yoko first flatly refuse to come to Bermuda, then stay for less than two days? Why was she now unwilling to speak to him on the telephone? Was she again punishing him for his sins with May Pang? Or for other sins he didn't even know about?

And then there was the steady drumbeat of gossip from the servants, nothing ever said in front of him, of course, but he couldn't help overhearing the little snippets of surreptitious chatter. Word was that Yoko was having an affair with "Sam." But there were two Sams, Havadtoy and Green, both interior decorators; John could never keep them straight. And there was that bit in Yoko's horoscope last month: "You should be extremely happy and even deeply involved in a new love affair because the Sun and Venus are passing through your angle of good fortune and romance."

What the fuck is that supposed to mean? Is Mother fucking one of her queer decorators?

These thoughts gave birth to *I'm Losing You*, a song about Mercury Retrograde in which John sings of disrupted communications and his inability to get Yoko on the telephone. *I'm Losing You* did make it on to *Double Fantasy*.

More than anything else, Yoko's visit had left John feeling guilty and heartsick. The relationship again seemed to be falling apart, and it was all his fault.

It was a gorgeous afternoon, not a cloud in the sky, when John sat on the porch behind Villa Undercliffe, looking out at Hamilton Harbor and eating the psilocybin mushrooms his servant had managed to smuggle through customs. Staring at the blue water, thinking of his selfishness towards Yoko and Sean, John began to cry. Then he wrote *Woman*, the song pouring from him whole. When he was finished, he again thanked God for the inspiration.

Beautiful Boy, both a tribute to Sean and to John's fantasy of an ideal family, was next. For the demo tape, he'd not yet written the most profound lyric (attributed by some to astrologer Patric Walker), an elegant twist on "the best-laid plans of mice and men." Instead, he mumbled something about "what the karma planned."

More songs followed at a white heat: *Girls and Boys*, for Sean, and *My Little Flower Princess*, for Yoko. The only reason *Girls and Boys* was not used on *Double Fantasy* was because it was too similar to Yoko's *Beautiful Boys*, which was used. Fifteen years later, Paul McCartney would transform *Girls and Boys* into *Real Love* for *The Beatles Anthology*.

My Little Flower Princess, a perfect *Double Fantasy* song, was never recorded in its entirety because John misplaced the lyric sheet and couldn't remember all the words. In it, he asks Yoko to forgive him because he can't replace her and he intends to spend the rest of his life thanking her and thanking her.

It was only after completing the demo tape that John realized *Double Fantasy* had to be a dialogue between him and Yoko, one of his songs followed by one of hers. He was so excited by the idea, he considered rushing back to the United States to record it immediately in Nashville. Then he decided that New York was the only place to do it. But the important thing was that his demo tape was complete. He could listen to it in the studio and draw inspiration from it.

John also knew that he could take nothing for granted. He'd been out of the music business for five years. He wasn't worried that people had forgotten him. He was worried they might remember all too well the headaches that he and Yoko had caused. It would be artistically and commercially suicidal, he thought, to go into the studio with the attitude that he was John Fuckin' Lennon and anything he came up with was guaranteed to go triple platinum. The situation was actually quite the opposite. He'd always had trouble getting airplay for his solo albums. *Plastic Ono Band,* his first and what he considered his best solo work, was the perfect example. Two of the finest songs, *Working Class Hero* and *I Found Out,* contained the words "fucking" and "cock." These words had to be bleeped out on the rare occasions that the songs were played on the radio. Other songs, like *Mother* and *God,* were considered too depressing and uncomfortably honest to play.

Yoko's aggressively noncommercial avant-garde material had even more trouble getting airplay. People hated her and her music and would be hesitant to even give it a listen. In 1973, when *Mind Games* was released, the airplay situation was nightmarish. Hostile program directors tossed the single in the garbage because it was "too long."

Now, in 1980, John feared that these same people would be put off by the family theme. He feared they were expecting him to make an important social statement. He feared that the LP would simply not live up to anybody's expectations.

John didn't want to make a statement on the album. His plan was to avoid controversy as much as possible. He didn't need more enemies. He already had enough.

Despite his concerns, John was delighted he'd accomplished what he'd set out to do. He'd arrived in Bermuda over a month ago, a wasted-looking, paranoid ex-Beatle. At Villa Undercliffe, he'd found his center. He'd created new music. Now, fit, tan, and rejuvenated, he was excited about going back into the studio. But before returning to New York he was going to have one last bit of fun; he was going to have his portrait painted with Sean.

MADONNA AND CHILD

AN ARTIST FROM NEW JERSEY, NANCY GOSNELL, WAS living nearby on the island. John, impressed by her Luthi family portrait hanging in the Villa Undercliffe living room, hired Gosnell to paint him and Sean. Inspired by the assignment, she threw herself into it, with father and son posing for her daily. She completed the portrait in less than a week, and it was exactly what John wanted. He loved it. Wearing a tank top and bathing suit and holding Sean in his lap, John looked overtly feminine; it was a 1980's interpretation of the Madonna and Child. Yoko loved it too and would hang it in her office in Studio One, a modern touch among the Egyptian antiques.

Before leaving Bermuda, John and Sean decided to go sailing one more time. They had an assistant charter a yacht. John dressed in white from head to toe for the occasion and carried a shoulder bag emblazoned with the logo of the New York public television station, WNET. He looked strangely like Peter Sellers, whose death that week had shocked him badly. Sean had a great time steering the boat out on the ocean. But the crew kept staring at John, making him edgy. He sat on deck chain-smoking.

John and Sean flew back to New York at the end of July. At the Bermuda airport, John had a bad time with customs. He'd spent a fortune on Front Street. There were a blizzard of forms to fill out, gawking crowds of tourists, customs agents demanding his autograph. But none of this mattered. He signed the autographs graciously. He was going home with new music. Everything was about to change in ways that he could hardly imagine and in ways that he could imagine all too clearly. A new life was about to begin, or rather, he was about to reclaim his old life—John Lennon, rock 'n' roll superstar.

Part III

THE
FINAL
DAYS

DOUBLE FANTASY

"'I've made my contribution to society and will never work again.'
Can you imagine me saying something as pompous as that? You can?!
Then fuck off!"—John Lennon, circa 1980

AND STILL JOHN CONTINUED TO CLIP THE *TOWN &*
Country horoscopes—Libra for him, Aquarius for Yoko.

Libra: When Venus your ruler is eclipsed by the Moon on
the 7th, there will no longer be any doubt in your mind about
where you are going professionally. You have a powerhouse of
creative talents. Saturn, entering your birth sign in September,
can only improve your lot.

Aquarius: You must accept partners and partnerships as
they are, and not find excuses for delaying decisions. When
Saturn moves into the sign of Libra in late September and
joins forces with Pluto, you could be destined to enjoy a
remarkable period of enlightening experiences and personal
fulfillment.

By the time John arrived in New York City at the end of July,
Yoko had already put out the word: We're going into the studio to
record an LP. But with no band and no record label, it seemed that
every musician, record company executive, and producer in town
was clamoring for a piece of the action. They flocked to the Dakota
to meet with Yoko in Studio One, under her favorable blue sky,
amidst the magical Egyptian antiques. They negotiated, talked of
music, and, most important, told Yoko their date and hour of birth,
which she subjected to numerological and zodiacal analysis.

As Yoko managed the Studio One turmoil, John stayed upstairs,
in Apartment 72, polishing his songs and playing with Sean.

AP/Wide World Photos

John Lennon and Yoko Ono arrive at The Hit Factory in
midtown Manhattan on August 22, 1980, two weeks into
the Double Fantasy recording sessions. By this time,
John had virtually given up writing in his journal
and was pouring all his energy into the music.

Occasionally he poked his head into the office to say hello to an old
acquaintance.

The *Double Fantasy* team was assembled in a matter of days.
Jack Douglas, who had been the engineer on *Imagine* and had since
produced groups like Aerosmith and Cheap Trick, was chosen to
produce the album because of his innate understanding of rock 'n'
roll and his sensitivity to Yoko's more avant-garde tastes.

The band, hand-picked by Douglas, was a collection of the best
studio musicians available: Hugh McCracken and Earl Slick on guitar, Tony Levin on bass, George Small on keyboards, Andy
Newmark on drums, and Arthur Jenkins on percussion. Scores of
background singers and horn players were also recruited. The
thought of stepping into the limelight was making John nervous
and insecure, and he felt the need to surround himself with an army.

As rehearsals began in the Dakota, the musicians were in a state
of shock. They couldn't believe they were working with John
Lennon. Everybody's fantasy had come true, and they just sat
around grinning at each other. The problem was that John was

making everybody uptight just by his presence, and they were making him uptight as well. To break the tension, Hugh McCracken began playing *I Want You*, one of John's songs from *Abbey Road*. John laughed. "That's the first song I ever wrote about Yoko," he said. "Most of my songs are about her, you know."

John and Hugh communicated well; their guitar exchanges were electrifying. John had a tendency to play in unusual keys and sometimes had trouble fitting in. Hugh would suggest other chords. John experimented. Progress was made.

On August 8, when they moved to the Hit Factory, a recording studio in midtown Manhattan, John virtually stopped writing on a daily basis. No more obsessive recording of every morsel of food he put in his mouth, or of every bowel movement, or of every time he jacked off, or of every one of Sean's mood swings. There was no more self-chastisement for smoking, or for failing to do yoga, or for eating sugar, or for drinking too much coffee. There was no more mention of the O, or the numbers, or the zodiac. Now the only thing he did was go to the Hit Factory to work on *Double Fantasy*. Some days he was so busy he wrote nothing, the first completely blank days since Sean's birth. All his energy was going into the LP, and they had to work fast. With no record contract, the Lennons were footing all the bills.

As work began on *Starting Over*, everybody sensed the significance of the moment.

"We've got ourselves a hit!" one of the background singers shouted.

John asked her if she was the voice of a singing cat in a popular cat food commercial.

"I wish," she said.

Then it was Yoko's turn with *I'm Your Angel*. Though she was nervous, her voice cracking, she still struggled through, with John and the musicians urging her on. She wasn't used to this kind of treatment; she was more accustomed to engineers and producers laughing at her screams and warbles, ridiculing her, walking out. Now everybody was pulling for her, because it was understood: without Yoko there would be no LP.

She got so nervous she asked a servant to bring her vodka in a water glass. She didn't want anybody to know she was drinking.

John, thinking the glass was full of water, took a sip and gasped.

"Are you drinking, Mother?" he asked.

Everybody laughed.

Eventually, Douglas had to splice together Yoko's song note by note, from countless takes.

There were other complications, too. Yoko's efforts to be "commercial" resulted in a number of extremely boring songs that even the most charitable people thought did not belong on the album. Jack Douglas was the only one willing to confront the issue. In particular, he wanted to cut *Beautiful Boys,* Yoko's tribute to John and Sean.

John wouldn't hear of it, and he demanded that the musicians come up with something, anything, to make the song more interesting. Inspired, they livened it up with provocative guitar work and improvised a classical-sounding melody.

Taking his cues from John, Douglas guided Yoko through each song. Sitting on the floor, he slapped out the beat on his thighs and on the floor.

As the session progressed, friction developed between the Lennons and Douglas over a contractual dispute; it was unclear if Douglas was entitled to three or five percent of *Double Fantasy.* Then he started showing up late for sessions, and John was furious. He was convinced that Douglas was playing games, fucking with his head. But he did nothing about it. When the album was complete, then Yoko would deal with him.

Every day the crew reported to the Hit Factory in the early evening. John was a tough boss and a perfectionist. Demanding total concentration from the musicians, he forbade anybody to smoke dope during the sessions. When he was ready to play, everybody had to be ready. "Get your cock in here!" he'd scream at anybody who wasn't.

Between takes, to maintain their energy level, the musicians munched on candy bars and honey graham crackers. They played till midnight, then broke for dinner, usually a feast ordered in from Mr. Chow on Eighth Avenue. At times John and Yoko retreated to a corner to sit quietly with their arms around each other. Occasionally a masseuse came to the studio to administer shiatsu to the Lennons.

Sometimes in the wee hours of the morning, Sean and his governess would show up and stay till dawn. It was Sean's first opportunity to watch Mommy and Daddy at work. He'd sit in John's lap in the control room and fall asleep.

John's entire schedule was out of whack; he was going to bed at 5 A.M.

Midway through the sessions, John had his shoulder-length hair cut in a short, conservative style. He was now a respectable family man and father and it was important that his image match the image projected on *Double Fantasy*. Forgoing the jeans and cowboy shirts he'd been wearing all along, he now came to the studio dressed in a black suit, white shirt and black tie.

A high school gospel choir was brought in to sing background vocals on Yoko's *Hard Times Are Over*. "My friends aren't going to believe I was recording with a Beatle!" one of the girls cried.

Despite all the enthusiasm and excitement, John was haunted by the fear that *Double Fantasy* would be mediocre, and as the sessions progressed, the fear grew worse. He began lashing out at everybody around him, particularly Fred Seaman, his gofer.

In the middle of a song that wasn't going well, John stopped playing. The trouble, he decided, was that he wasn't wearing a hat. The correct hat would fix everything, and Lennon dispatched Seaman to the Dakota to retrieve it. A half hour later, he returned with a hat. John went nuts. Not only had the hapless assistant taken too much time, but he'd brought back the wrong hat.

"Stupid fucking fool!" he screamed. "What do I pay you for? Can't you do anything right? Haven't you got a brain in your fucking head? Now go bring me the right hat!"

It took nine days to record 22 tracks, 14 of which would be used on *Double Fantasy*. John was astonished by how smoothly everything went and of course he praised the Lord: *Thank You. Thank you. Thank you.*

Yoko was already talking about touring and using Phil Spector to produce the next album. Then it dawned on John exactly what was happening. After five years of isolation and relative privacy, they were about to step into the center of a frenzy that would resemble Beatlemania. He couldn't believe how quickly his world was changing, and he was frightened.

MEDIA BLITZ

Libra: There seems to be no doubt in your mind that you are about to lead a more independent and complete life. This is because you have already begun to feel the influence of the powerful planet Saturn which enters your birth sign on September 21. Be prepared to take full responsibility for yourself and face up to important facts and situations.

Aquarius: Remember that your own ruler Uranus, together with Mars, is sitting at the midheaven point of your solar chart. The most important benefit you should enjoy is fewer feuds over finances. Then as time goes by you should be able to prove that you have a mind bursting with seemingly outrageous plans, many of which could be money spinners.

THE SECOND WEEK OF SEPTEMBER, JOHN AND YOKO granted interviews to *Newsweek* and *Playboy*. It was the first time since 1975 that either one had met with a reporter, and their defenses were down; they felt they were too open. But they quickly honed their message to the media: John was a househusband. He'd spent the past five years bringing up baby and baking bread while Yoko, whom he loved very much, ran the business.

Thus began a flurry of interviews.

John enjoyed speaking with Robert Hillburn from *The Los Angeles Times.* He also met with Jonathan Cott, the *Rolling Stone* reporter who happened to be one of the only critics to praise John's first album with Yoko, comparing *Unfinished Music #1: Two Virgins* to the work of John Cage.

For the rest of the week, John and Yoko did nothing but talk to the press, work on mixing and remixing the LP, eat, and sometime after dawn, go to sleep.

That weekend, totally exhausted, the album progressing well, the Lennons stayed in bed and cancelled all interviews. John had had enough for a while and besides, it gave him pleasure to blow off reporters.

GEFFEN'S THE ONE

BY MID-SEPTEMBER THE LENNONS STILL HADN'T DECIDED on a record company. They considered the possibility of forming their own, but with the Apple nightmare still all too real, that idea was quickly squelched. Everybody wanted to put out their album, but there was nobody they could trust completely. Still, somebody had to do it; there was no avoiding it.

David Geffen, whose newly formed record label had yet to put out an album, had recently managed to sign Elton John and Donna Summer. For what it was worth, Geffen had a good reputation. He was also just over five feet tall, and Yoko liked that. He couldn't intimidate her with his height. Geffen knew John from hanging out with him during the 1974 *Rock 'n' Roll* sessions in Los Angeles. Like John, he'd gotten out of the music business in 1975.

Geffen met with Yoko in Studio One.

"What do you want?" she asked him.

"I want to put out your record," he said.

"Everybody wants to put out our record. What can you do for us? You haven't even put out a record yet."

"We've got a great company."

Geffen agreed to all of Yoko's demands without even hearing the album. Yoko took his numbers, did his astrological chart. Everything came out to her satisfaction. John met with Geffen; they chatted about old times and hit it off.

Within a matter of days, it was agreed that Geffen was the one. A simple contract was drawn up and, on September 22, signed. Geffen then listened to *Double Fantasy* for the first time, and he was blown away.

OCTOBER 9

Libra: Now is a time for action, not deliberation. You have had the whole of 1980 to decide what you want out of life and how your talents and skills can best be employed. Now you must act. This is a period of expansion and fulfillment, and you must not fail to see that it is up to you alone to decide what is right for you. Now it's not really money and security that count but your own self-esteem and spiritual growth.

Aquarius: Mars is too close to Uranus, your ruler, in that part of your solar chart related to prestige and standing. This will affect how people in positions of authority consider you. Either apologize and retract this October or you could be out in the cold.

IT WAS JOHN AND SEAN'S BIRTHDAY. LAST YEAR, THERE WERE no deadlines, only time. Having just returned from another extended stay in Japan, John had spent the morning alone in his bedroom. He was 39, getting ready for life to begin at 40. Since 1966, when he recorded *Sergeant Pepper*, everything had passed in the blink of an eye, and that was frightening. *It was 13 years ago today....* Staring aimlessly out the window at Central Park West, he recalled a quote that he attributed to George Orwell, author of *1984:* "At 50 everyone has the face they deserve." He was looking forward to 50.

Last year there had been a blow-out bash for John and Sean at Tavern on the Green, the opulent, overpriced tourist restaurant in Central Park that John could see from his bedroom window. He was grateful to Yoko for arranging the party. Everybody was invited, including half the neighbors from the Dakota, one of whom, Warner LeRoy, owned the restaurant. Clowns, magicians and fire-eaters circulated through the crowd, under fantastic emerald-green, ruby-red, and sapphire-blue chandeliers. As the entertainers delighted the children with their well-rehearsed antics, John thoroughly enjoyed pigging out at the buffet table on the wide assortment of cakes and pies. It was a perfect afternoon, he decided.

John went home feeling good. Awaiting him was a telegram from George Martin, the former Beatles producer, and a letter from his aunt Mimi. John was pleasantly surprised that Martin remembered his birthday. But elation turned to rage as he read the letter from Mimi; as usual, it was filled with criticism. Though their tempestuous relationship had mellowed now that they were separated by an ocean, it could still, at the drop of a hat, explode with violent emotions. Ever since John was a teenager, living with Mimi at Mendips, his aunt had adamantly disapproved of his lifestyle. When upset, she had had a nasty tendency to throw things at him.

John had dashed off a reply. Complaining that Mimi never liked any of his friends, he informed her that he'd not lost his common sense and that his songs weren't written for Victorians. He said that he was glad he didn't have to count on people like her to buy his music because if he did, he'd be broke and probably still living with her in Liverpool. (He never mailed the letter.)

Again Lennon began to dwell on how quickly his life was flying by, and it filled him with despair. So he'd snorted some heroin to kill the pain, then prayed to God for the willpower not to do it again. The lyrics for a song, *Life Begins at 40*, poured from him. Later, he'd sing it with Yoko, recording the duet on tape.

Now it was October 9, 1980, the "BIG 4-O." (The LITTLE 5 for Sean.) John woke up feeling deadline pressure over *Double Fantasy*. He sat in bed listening to birthday announcements on the radio, surprised that both John Entwistle, the bass player from The Who, and Jackson Browne shared his birthday.

The Lennons and their staff celebrated quietly in the Dakota kitchen. Playing the holy fool, John put on a dunce-like birthday hat that said "40" in block letters. He sat at the table with Sean, cutting the cake, blowing out the candles, making wishes, opening presents. Then they both kissed Yoko, who had remained on the telephone the entire time, monitoring the progress of *Double Fantasy*'s editing and mixing.

Outside on Central Park West and on 72nd Street, the fans had massed early, as they did every October 9. Spurred by the knowledge that a new album was due imminently, the crowd, bigger and noisier than usual, chanted "Happy birthday, John! Happy birthday, Sean!" and even "Happy birthday, Yoko!"

John sent them candy and balloons. Later in the afternoon, Sean went with his nanny, Helen, to the roof of the Dakota to watch the spectacle. The fans spotted him.

"Where's John?" they shouted.

"He's sleeping," Sean replied. "He can't come."

John watched from his bedroom window as skywriters wrote across the cloudless sky: "HAPPY BIRTHDAY JOHN + SEAN LOVE YOKO."

For reasons obscure even to John, Yoko had decided to move the *Double Fantasy* operation from the Hit Factory to its arch-competitor, the Record Plant. That night the Lennons went to the Record Plant and worked till dawn on the final editing and remixing. They learned that *Double Fantasy* had been chosen by *Rolling Stone* as one of the top ten albums for 1980. John was pleased. Never before had one of his LP's been honored before it was even completed. Now he just wanted to make sure that it was out before the end of the year.

COMPLETION

BY OCTOBER 18, *DOUBLE FANTASY* WAS COMPLETELY remixed; only the mastering remained. The last song finished was *Cleanup Time*, and Yoko did that entirely on her own. John was astonished but happy. He reluctantly admitted that he couldn't have done a better job himself.

For the past few days, he'd been too exhausted to go to the studio. He'd stayed in his room, thinking that they'd never be able to finish the album without him. Deep down, he knew that the completion of *Double Fantasy* was more than just the completion of another project—it was the end of a phase of his life, and he wasn't sure that he wanted it to end. But this was really the story of his life; he was incapable of finishing anything unless somebody put a gun to his head.

The November issue of *Esquire* came in the mail that week. John couldn't help but notice it because he was the cover story: *John Lennon's Private Life: A Madcap Mystery Tour. In search of the Beatle who spent two decades seeking true love and cranial bliss only to discover cows, daytime television and Palm Beach real estate.* The table of contents said of the article, written by Lawrence Shames, "A literary gumshoe sent to stalk the elusive Walrus finds that the missing Beatle is nowhere, man." According to this scathing investigative satire, assembled from information available on the public record, Lennon was now an inaccessible, semi-retired 40-year-old businessman with $150 million.

It's all bullshit, thought John.

ECSTASY

WHEN THE ALBUM WAS COMPLETED, JOHN, FEELING AS IF he'd just returned from the other side of the world, recuperated in the womb of the Dakota. He was functioning on adrenal reserves, and his internal clock was totally screwed up. He slept all day and sat up all night in the morning room. He didn't know what to do next.

Starting Over, the single, released before the album, was all over the radio by October 21. At first John was ecstatic. He discussed with Yoko the possibility of going right back into the studio to put together an LP of *Double Fantasy* outtakes. These would have a much harder edge and would be guaranteed to freak out everybody. Indeed, he thought, he'd release *Serve Yourself* right on the heels of *Beautiful Boy,* and nobody would know what to make of it. Same old Crazy John.

LIFE AFTER
DOUBLE FANTASY

Libra: These are hectic and decisive days for Libra subjects, not only because of unexpected developments at work that affect your income and security, but mainly due to changes going on in your personal life. Venus, your ruler, will be in Libra until November 23, adding its weight to Jupiter, Saturn and Pluto. Venus is a subtle planet but now more than ever, it makes you realize that you have no alternative than to follow the dictates of your heart. This may quite easily force you to change your lifestyle, but above all convince you that a great deal has to be discarded now if you are to find the happiness and fulfillment you desire and deserve.

Aquarius: You can't wait to move on and explore new avenues and opportunities. Four planets in the sympathetic sign of Libra indicate that this is a wonderfully stimulating and enlightening period for you. When the Sun is close to your ruling planet on November 18, there is likely to be a monstrous upheaval. However, it's important that you continue to look outwards and beyond your immediate situation and day to day problems, because Saturn in Libra over the next couple of years can and will provide you with fantastic outlets for your creative and artistic abilities.

AP/Wide World Photos

Muhammad Ali (center) greets Yoko and John at a party at the Kennedy Center in Washington, D.C. The event honored Jimmy Carter on the eve of his inauguration as President in January 1977. When Carter lost his bid for re-election to Ronald Reagan in 1980, Lennon speculated that Reagan would be assassinated and the country would fall into the clutches of the vice president, former CIA director George Bush.

O N NOVEMBER 4, "ERECTION DAY"—A PUN HE COULD never resist—as America overwhelmingly banished Jimmy Carter from the White House (John and Yoko had attended his inaugural ball), Lennon speculated that Ronald Reagan would be assassinated and the United States would fall into the malevolent clutches of former CIA director George Bush.

On Sunday afternoon, November 16, Julian called John. It was the last time they'd ever speak. Julian, as usual, told his father that he was broke again and needed money. The conversation was strained and pissed John off, making him wonder again whether money was the only thing Julian wanted from him. John felt used. Yet, after he hung up the phone, he continued thinking about his son and found himself caught up in a nostalgic Liverpudlian reverie.

Then, with the release of his LP imminent, he forgot about Julian.

Double Fantasy officially went on sale the next day; WPLJ, the New York radio station, announced a *Double Fantasy* listening party to preview the album.

"That'll be fun," he told the servants. "Let's tape it."

Within days the entire album was being played everywhere, all the time, but John's initial ecstasy dissolved into despair. His worst fears had been realized. Compared to Springsteen and The Cars, *Double Fantasy* didn't make it; it *was* mediocre.

The problem was that John had been doing rock 'n' roll for 25 years, and that was way too long. He was sick of it. What was the point? He'd never be hot again. There was nothing to work for. The idea of recording and touring simply didn't excite him. He didn't want to do it anymore. But what else was there to do? Maybe, he thought, it was best to drop out of sight again and leave it all up to Yoko. Let the media focus on her and forget about him. He was tired of the pressure. He wanted to be left alone.

But life at the Dakota continued as always. Reporters came and went. The *Playboy* interview hit the newsstands. *Double Fantasy* steadily climbed the charts. John was amazed. Apparently he was the only one who found it mediocre. He received word that Keith Richards, the Rolling Stones' guitarist, had bought a copy. It was kind of nice to have another hit LP, he thought. Still, something wasn't quite right. Something was missing. There was always something missing, and maybe, as he said in *Serve Yourself,* it was his mother.

Sometimes, when John was sitting in the morning room, looking out at Central Park, his thoughts turned to the afterlife. More and more frequently he caught himself daydreaming of the eternal bliss that lay beyond. Yet he certainly didn't want to die. Too many things were going well, particularly his relationship with Sean. John would read to him at bedtime. Reading to Sean made John happy.

But haunted by the question of what to do next, John longed for something—an answer. Yoko wasn't around anymore. The only time John ever saw her was at seven in the morning, when she woke up. Then she went to the Record Plant to work on her new single, *Walking on Thin Ice.* She was determined to have it out by Christmas. There would be a video to go with it, of course, and

John was required for the lovemaking scene. He didn't particularly want to do something quasi-pornographic in front of a camera, but Yoko insisted. So John gritted his teeth and performed according to her direction.

In many ways, John enjoyed his solitude, though he did miss having Yoko around.

Just before Thanksgiving, John and Yoko met with Ringo and his fiancee, Barbara Bach, in their suite at the Plaza Hotel. Nude photos of Barbara were in the same issue of *Playboy* as John and Yoko's interview. John had studied the pictures, but it was not until he saw her in person that he was taken by Barbara's beauty.

John and Yoko sat with Ringo talking business, as Barbara tended to her brood of kids, one of whom appeared to have some kind of neuromuscular disease. John couldn't help thinking about the old days in Liverpool when, as a teenager, he was famous for his grotesque impressions of spastics and cripples. He'd run up to them in the street and make horrible faces.

Ringo was telling John about his upcoming album, the yet-to-be-titled *Stop and Smell the Roses*. It was in an embryonic stage and Ringo needed more material fast. John agreed to write a couple of songs for him, and Ringo was delighted.

YOKO ONLY

Libra: Never have you been so active, positive and on form. If there was ever a time in your life when fortune beckoned you to stand up and be counted, this is it.

Aquarius: Plans, projects and new possibilities are all clearly spotlighted by planetary aspects now. The 2nd, 23rd and 31st will be days of conflict, argument and tears before bedtime. A whole new life appears to be yours for the asking.

BY DECEMBER, *DOUBLE FANTASY* WAS IN THE TOP TEN in all the trade magazines; *Starting Over*, the single, was number four. Naturally, John praised the Lord.

Wednesday, December 3, *The Soho News* appeared with a photo of Yoko on its cover along with the headline "Yoko Only." The Lennons were sitting in bed when a servant brought them a copy, handing it to Yoko. But John was more excited about it than she was and snatched it out of her hand, intent on reading it first. He then dispatched the servant to buy 100 more copies and have one framed.

Yoko had been working obsessively on her *Thin Ice* single and video. With *The Soho News* saying that she was now hot in her own right, John was suddenly inspired again. He began going with her to the studio every day, adding guitar to *Thin Ice*.

"You've got a hit, Mother," he predicted.

Now John, too, was pushing for the single to be out by Christmas, and he also wanted Yoko to release a solo album titled *Discono*. But David Geffen told them to slow down. He wanted to do it right; that meant taking out an ad for Yoko in the trades.

John received word that *Starting Over* had sold over 200,000 copies in the United Kingdom. He couldn't believe it. He had prayed for sales like that in the UK but never thought it would actually happen. This almost made up for the horrible way Yoko had been treated in England, which was the primary reason they'd left the country.

WEEKEND

SATURDAY MORNING, DECEMBER 6, SEAN WENT TO A farm in Pennsylvania with Helen, his governess.

Around 9 A.M., John phoned Mimi. He told her he was planning to come to England and that he would see her soon.

Later, John got to thinking about *Two Virgins*, the now extremely hard-to-find album he'd recorded with Yoko in 1968, on the first night they made love. It was really an avant-garde, aggressively noncommercial precursor to *Double Fantasy*, wasn't it? On the cover were the two of them stark naked—cock, pussy...everything. Yet the uproar over this harmless bit of fun was nearly as bad as the "bigger than Jesus" controversy. Now John realized that it would inevitably be a major collector's item. It was already selling for two hundred bucks and the price was bound to double. He dispatched a servant to buy as many copies of *Two Virgins* as he could find, then stopped into La Fortuna for an afternoon cappuccino before having his hair cut. Back at the Dakota, he was informed that *Kiss Kiss Kiss*, Yoko's B-side of *Starting Over*, was being played constantly at discos.

John and Yoko ate dinner at Mr. Chow, then met at the Record Plant with Andy Peebles of the BBC for yet another interview.

Sunday, December 7, John rested. He didn't venture outside. It was quiet.

1 2 / 8 / 8 0

MONDAY MORNING, DECEMBER 8, ANNIE LEIBOVITZ OF *Rolling Stone* came to the Dakota for a photo session. Late that afternoon, when they had finished posing for the now-famous shots of nude-John-in-the-fetal-position-with-Yoko, they spoke with Dave Sholin of the RKO Radio Network. John's tone in this interview, which was to be his last, was strikingly similar to that of his pre–*Double Fantasy* diaries:

"I get up at six, go to the kitchen, get a cup of coffee, cough a little, have a cigarette, papers arrive at seven," he said. "Sean gets up at 7:20, 25. I oversee his breakfast. I don't cook it anymore. Got fed up with that one. But I make sure I know what he's eating...."

After the interview, the Lennons left for the Record Plant to work on *Thin Ice*.

A note about this recording session was the last entry in Lennon's diary, a couple of words scrawled on the run.

When he returned to the Dakota at 11 P.M., the time in England was 4 A.M., the date December 9.

THE BEST IS YET TO BE

JOHN AND YOKO BELIEVED THAT THEY WERE THE reincarnation of Victorian poets Robert Browning and Elizabeth Barrett Browning. And in the end, on the very last page of his diary, Lennon copied a verse from Browning's curiously titled *Rabbi Ben Ezra*, which the poet had dedicated to his wife. John was so enchanted by Browning's lines that he used them in his own song, recorded during the *Double Fantasy* sessions but included instead on *Milk and Honey*.

The lines were:

Grow old along with me!
The best is yet to be.

The Coda

1980–1981

THE CITY
ON THE EDGE
OF TIME

JOHN LENNON WAS SHOT TO DEATH DECEMBER 8, 1980, at 11 P.M. in the archway of the Dakota in New York City. To begin to understand why, it's necessary to look west, to a small volcanic island in the Pacific called Oahu.

Imagine Mark David Chapman in Honolulu, Hawaii, a sweltering, neon-lit city on the edge of the American Empire, on the edge of time, the last spot of Western Civilization the sun passes over on its way to the International Dateline and...tomorrow.

At 6 P.M. on a weeknight in Honolulu, Chapman walks aimlessly around Kukui Plaza near his apartment in the downtown area. People are just getting home from work, settling down to dinner. It could be December, or March, or July. It doesn't really matter. Every day's the same. Every day in Honolulu is August, a New York August. And while it's dinner time here, it's midnight on the East Coast and back home in Georgia.

Everything in Honolulu is disjointed—California cool meets the sprawling metropolises of Asia: Saigon, Seoul, Singapore, Tokyo, Bangkok, Manila. It's an excellent place for a tropical vacation if you've got the dough. That's why he came here originally, to see Waikiki, the dream destination of ten million tourists. But Honolulu is no place for a complete outsider to live. Unfortunately, Chapman *has* chosen to live here. He has come to Hawaii seeking a new life, a new job, a new beginning. He has managed to find a wife—an older Japanese woman, Gloria Abe, who was his travel agent. But beyond Gloria, what he finds is...nothing.

Imagine Mark David Chapman in the supermarket. Prices of the basic necessities are out of whack—*two dollars for a fucking quart of milk?!* How long can anybody live on the three affordable items: macadamia nuts, coffee and fresh pineapple?

The wages are low, the climate oppressive, and as Chapman knows as well as anybody, the mental hospitals (not to mention the prisons) are overflowing. But there is a church and a hostess bar on every block, Jesus Christ and Mary Magdalen always beckoning. Your choice, Mister Chapman, born again or traditional Asian blowjob?

Weekdays at noon, he walks the streets searching for a job, searching for something, just searching, the sun a ball of fire in the sky. His exposed flesh feels as if it's roasting. *Mad dogs and Englishmen. What am I doing here?* He's a stranger in a place that makes no sense to him, surrounded by heartbreaking beauty. Honolulu—what a place to lose your mind.

March 1980: Mark David Chapman—already seeing himself as the embodiment of Holden Caulfield, the young, slightly mad, somewhat cowardly, hypocrisy-hating hero of J. D. Salinger's *The Catcher in the Rye*—wanders into the Honolulu Public Library just to get out of the sun. Why not? He's got a library card. It's air-conditioned. It's free. And he likes to read—especially that Salinger book; there's nothing like it in the world. In fact, he keeps reading *Catcher* over and over; it's a bit of an obsession, really. It's like reading his own biography. Freaky stuff. How can any book be so good and so true? In that book, between the blood-red covers, he sees hope and salvation. He sees his own identity. That's why he gives it to Gloria. Read it, he says, and you will know me.

Chapman wanders the aisles of the library, browsing, looking for nothing in particular. Then his eye falls upon the spine of a book, *John Lennon: One Day at a Time*. It calls out to him from the dusty shelf: Ah, synchronicity. He takes the book to a table, where he begins to thumb through it—not reading really, just looking at the pictures, which he finds very disturbing. Images of John Lennon sear his brain.

The book is by Anthony Fawcett, one of Lennon's former personal assistants, who was with the ex-Beatle prior to 1975, just before he chose to go into seclusion. It's a flattering portrait of the musician, but this is not the message that Chapman is receiving.

All he sees are the photographs, and they fill him with confusion and a murderous rage. What is John Lennon doing in New

York? Why isn't he living in England, where he belongs, like the rest of the damn Beatles?

He sees Lennon, looking like some degenerate French monarch from the 18th century, in the luxurious Dakota, a building that seems to him like the wicked witch's castle in *The Wizard of Oz*, his favorite movie. And at that moment he knows that something he's suspected for a very long time is God's own truth: John Lennon is a phony son of a bitch, just the sort of guy Chapman's alter ego, Holden Caulfield, would despise. Lyrics flitter across his roiling brain: *All you need is love...Imagine no possessions....* Yeah, right. No possessions for me. Cause you have everything.

At last he sees the light: Lennon's music—the music he once loved so much—is pure propaganda. Not a word of it is true. Lennon is a corrupt, debased liar, a rich businessman just like all the others. He used his music to ruin lives—*my life*—to mislead an entire generation. The ex-Beatle exudes phoniness; it radiates off him like heat.

The envy and jealousy that surge through Chapman's body and mind are too much to bear. While Lennon is happily residing in New York City with more fame than is imaginable, and with every material comfort money can buy, he is stuck in wretched Honolulu, three-quarters out of his mind, living in turmoil with nothing. It just isn't fair that one person should have so much while most people have so little.

Later in the week Chapman returns to the library, this time to play records. Normally, he listens to Todd Rundgren, Lennon's musical arch-enemy. He thinks Rundgren's a genius, far superior to Lennon. But among the library's extensive selection, Chapman is able to locate a chestnut he hasn't heard in some time: *Plastic Ono Band*, Lennon's first solo release after leaving the Beatles. As he sits alone in the cubicle with headphones pressed to his ears, the music of *God* fills his head, providing a soundtrack for those photos he saw the other day: Lennon in pornographic splendor. Chapman, who believes in the power and love of Jesus Christ, is infuriated that Lennon doesn't believe in God, or Jesus...just Yoko and himself. *Who does he think he is?*

YOUNG MAN WITH A GOAL

I**T WOULD BE INSANE TO SUGGEST THAT MARK DAVID** Chapman was a stable, healthy human being before arriving in Honolulu from his home in the suburbs of Atlanta, Georgia. But something did happen to him during the three years he spent in Hawaii. Something in Honolulu pushed him over the edge.

The tendency, for anybody who's read about the matter over the years, is to picture Chapman at midnight, naked and stoned on acid, in his downtown Honolulu apartment, strumming an acoustic guitar while blasting over his stereo system *Piggies* and *Revolution 9* from the Beatles' "White Album." He summons the spirits of Satan, the Manson Family, bloody helter skelter, and all that is unholy. And, of course, he chants, "John Lennon must die...." It is his mantra. In the next room, his devoutly Christian wife, Gloria, who loves him dearly, is sleeping fitfully, her husband's chanting and guitar playing, and the Beatles' music, at the edge of her consciousness. She thinks she's having a bad dream, and in fact, she is, worse than she can even imagine.

This somehow satisfying image—satisfying because it seems to neatly explain so many things—is not terribly far from the truth. The truth entails only a slight refocusing of the lens.

Chapman, for one thing, had stopped taking LSD in 1969, when he was 14 years old. And when he did drop acid back then, *Magical Mystery Tour* was the album he preferred to listen to. More important, it is Lennon's picture on the inside cover of *Sergeant Pepper,* and his voice on *Lucy in the Sky with Diamonds,* that make Chapman ultimately realize that the Beatle must die. And it is Satan alone whom he begs for the power to kill John Lennon. Fleeting thoughts of Manson and the "White Album" will come later, in a "synchronistic" manner. Everything comes in a synchronistic manner to Mark David Chapman.

It's a veritable epiphany for Chapman the moment he realizes that it is his holy mission to murder Lennon. He ceases to hurt inside; his mind grows quiet. He feels sane and clear, which is something he's never felt before—ever. The transformation is immediate and magical. Mark David Chapman, in the time it takes to listen to a song, has gone from a loser with no sense of self to a young man with a goal and an identity. And as John Lennon would have been the first to confirm, a young man with a goal can accomplish anything. He can rock the world.

WHAT WOULD HOLDEN DO?

CHAPMAN HAS BEEN IN HAWAII SINCE MAY 1977 AND during that time he's failed at everything, even suicide. He can't even snuff himself with some simple carbon monoxide poisoning from the exhaust of his car. He's been in and out of mental hospitals, and in and out of menial jobs—hospital orderly, security guard. Through it all, he is consumed by a desire to be recognized as *somebody*, and he continues to grope for an identity in the only way he knows how: He runs up enormous debts by spending weekends with his wife in expensive Waikiki beachfront hotels, and by renting luxury cars. But this doesn't give him an identity; it gives him bills he can't afford to pay. And all he feels in his whirling, out-of-control mind is anger on a good day, blinding rage on a bad one.

But now that he has a goal, certain things begin to fall into place. Significantly, after an absence of several months, the "Little People" return. The Little People are an entire civilization—men, women, and children who, for as long as Chapman can remember, have lived in a city in his head, and in the walls of his room. As a child, he'd ruled over them, a benevolent dictator, his image projected on a television screen as he gave speeches. When he was ten years old, in 1965, he'd play *Meet the Beatles* for them when they were good. The Little People loved him for it.

As an adult, they have helped him make decisions, usually of a financial nature. *Shall I buy this painting I love, or shall I pay off my credit card?* Now he has to make the biggest decision he's ever made in his life. If he is to carry out his plan, he needs the Little People to cooperate. He tells them that he wants to murder John Lennon. Since Chapman is marginally more mature than he was as an eight-year-old, the government of the Little People is now run as a democracy—he has given power to the Little People. They overrule his decision. "Don't do it," they beg him at a board meeting. "It will only cause pain for the people you care about, your wife, your mother."

Chapman strongly disagrees with the Little People. Don't they understand he *needs* to murder Lennon? They understand it, all right, but they can't condone it. They are good people—Christians—and they want no part of his diabolical plan. The Little People are left with no choice but to abandon him.

Chapman is now on his own. He knows it won't be easy to murder a celebrity who lives six thousand miles away in a city he once visited briefly, in the seventh grade. To commit world-class mayhem takes planning, organization...inspiration. Primarily, he needs money, he needs a gun, and he needs to get to New York.

The money isn't difficult to come by. Chapman fancies himself an art afficionado. For years he's been acquiring paintings, lithographs, *objets d'art.* First he sells a $5,000 Salvador Dali gold plaque, originally purchased with a loan from his father-in-law. Then, with a $2,500 loan from his mother, he purchases a Norman Rockwell print titled "Triple Self Portrait." Shrewdly, he's able to sell it to a collector for a good profit. His money problems are solved, no thanks to the Little People.

Inspiration, too, comes easily. For hours on end, while his wife sleeps, Chapman sits alone in his apartment listening to all his old Beatles and John Lennon albums. The lies in the music drive him wild.

He chants his mantra: *The phony must die says the Catcher in the Rye.*

He understands now with perfect clarity that if he wipes John Lennon from the face of the earth, he'll have nothing more to worry about. He will be at peace with himself. In fact, he's convinced that he will literally become Holden Caulfield, and there will be a new chapter added to *The Catcher in the Rye:* Chapter 27, his chapter, the chapter that will be written in Lennon's blood. But for this prophecy to come to pass, the Beatle, of course, must die.

In Honolulu, as in the rest of America, it's every man and woman's constitutional right to own a handgun. Mark David Chapman is no exception. On October 27, 1980, he walks into a gun store, identifies himself as a security guard and says he needs a gun for protection. The clerk, Robin Ono—synchronicity—shows him a .38-caliber revolver. It feels good in his hand, just the right weight, and he pays for it with cash—$169. Of course, he has to fill out a gun-permit application; it's the law. But it's a mere formality. He does the paperwork in a nearby police station. One of the questions on the application is, *Have you ever been hospitalized for mental illness?* Chapman lies, but nobody bothers to do a background check.

The next day Chapman signs out as "John Lennon" at his security guard job in a luxury housing complex. He tells his wife he's going to New York City to get his head together. She voices no protest. It is a wife's duty to obey her husband. As it says in the Bible.

On October 29, Chapman boards a flight to New York City, his gun in his suitcase, checked through into the baggage compartment.

He spends the next week in New York. It's odd, yet enjoyable, being in the city for the first time since seventh grade. Chapman likes the Big Apple. From his obsessive readings of *Catcher,* he feels as if he knows the city well. Just like Holden Caulfield, he checks into a hotel. First he spends two nights at the luxurious Waldorf Astoria, then moves to the Olcott, on 72nd Street, right next door to the Dakota. Finally, as his money begins to run low, he checks into the YMCA, just nine blocks from the Dakota.

The weather is good for mid-autumn, crisp and comfortably cool. He spends his afternoons hanging out in front of the Dakota, hoping to see Lennon. He befriends the Dakota doormen and the "troupies" who keep a daily vigil there, hoping to spot a Lennon, any Lennon, or a member of his staff, and exchange a few words. "Is John Lennon home today?" Chapman asks various people. The doormen are evasive and tell him nothing, or they say that Lennon's traveling. But the troupies, thinking he's harmless, just another fan, are friendly and share with him everything they know about Lennon's schedule. It doesn't do Chapman any good. Though one of the hard-core fans, who goes by the name Jude, actually introduces him to Sean and his governess as they return from a walk in the park, he never sees Lennon himself.

To pass the long, lonely hours in New York when he isn't camped outside the Dakota, Chapman, like any other tourist—or like Holden Caulfield—takes in a few Broadway shows and eats lavish dinners at good restaurants. In the strictest confidence, he tells the people he meets—the troupies and a woman he manages to pick up in Central Park—that soon he's going to do something that they will hear about. He's going to be a celebrity. It disturbs him that they don't seem to understand what he's saying...or they don't believe him.

One afternoon when he's strolling through Central Park, just for good measure—just to be like Holden—he asks a cop where the ducks in the lake go when winter comes. The cop walks away without answering. Chapman feels slighted. He wanted to explain the joke to him, tell the cop that he's just like Holden Caulfield.

Despite lurking in front of the Dakota at all hours of the day and night, Chapman has still not seen Lennon, and his frustration is building. Then, on November 4, after eight days in New York, he suddenly gets the feeling that he's going to see Lennon imminently, and when he does, he'll have to kill him. The only problem is that he has no ammunition for his gun, and he soon discovers that it's legally impossible to buy bullets in New York City.

On November 5, he flies to Georgia, where he hooks up with an old friend, Dana Reeves, who is now a sheriff's deputy. Chapman explains to Reeves that he's going to be spending time in New York and he needs to protect himself from muggers, vicious people. Ordinary bullets won't do the job. He needs hollow-point bullets, something with real stopping power, something that will rip a man to pieces upon impact. You can't be too careful, says Chapman.

Reeves trusts his old friend and gives him what he needs—the hollow-point bullets that Chapman will inevitably use to kill Lennon. Then Reeves takes Chapman out into the woods for a few hours of target practice with his .38. Chapman isn't very good at first, so Reeves gives him a few pointers, teaches him the "combat stance"—crouched, holding the pistol with both hands. As the session progresses, Chapman displays a definite talent for marksmanship, hitting his target with consistency, the bullets grouped closely together.

With the ammunition and gun in his suitcase, again checked through to the baggage compartment, Chapman, on November 8, returns to New York City, flying first class. It is on this flight that he sees the *Esquire* magazine with Lennon on the cover. The picture startles him, calls to him from the magazine rack. *Synchronicity.* He reads the article, entranced. Lennon is depicted as an isolated multi-millionaire businessman who's become the antithesis of everything he once represented. His life, traceable only through material on the public record, has been reduced to a series of deeds and contracts. The article paints a shattering portrait of a man who is what he possesses. And, as if he needs it, the *Esquire* article gives Chapman that one last bit of motivation and inspiration. *Lennon must die says the Catcher in the Rye.*

But Lennon will live for another month. Despite his patient stalking, the endless hours spent waiting outside the Dakota, Chapman never sees the Beatle. On November 12, he calls Gloria, back in Hawaii. She's thrilled to hear from him, and half out of her mind with worry.

"I know you're not going to believe me but I was going to kill John Lennon."

"Oh, Mark, I do believe you. Please come home."

Chapman boards a flight at Newark airport, goes home for the last time.

But the demons will not be easily silenced. Eighteen days of anguish and emotional turmoil pass in Honolulu. Chapman cannot forget about Lennon's phoniness, his betrayal. He cannot forget about his own holy mission, his goal, the very reason he was put on this earth. He knows he has no choice but to go back and finish what he started. It's early December, coming on Christmas, Christmas in New York, the period of time in which *The Catcher in the Rye* takes place. He knows he has to return to the city to fulfill the prophecy, to write Chapter 27 in Lennon's blood. He still has some money left. He tells his mother, who now also lives in Hawaii, that he's going back to take care of some unfinished business.

"You're not going to do anything *funny,* Mark, are you?" she asks.

Certainly not, he says, and boards a flight to New York City. Indeed, nothing funny at all about what needs to be done.

Chapman returns to the West Side YMCA, a budgetary measure; he's determined not to run out of cash before completing his mission. Through the thin walls of his cubicle he hears the disgusting sounds of two men making love. *Oh, dear God, there are perverts everywhere. This is exactly what happened to Holden in his hotel.*

Not exactly. Holden was amused by the "perverts" he watched through his window in the Edmont Hotel. Chapman is anything but amused by his YMCA neighbors. They drive him into a fit of rage. He wants to kill them immediately, start firing his gun wildly through the wall until the sounds of perversion cease and there is only blessed quiet. But he manages to gain control of his emotions. He knows if he kills anybody now, then he won't be able to kill John Lennon. The game will be over, the prophecy unfulfilled.

To escape the perverts, Chapman packs his bags and moves to a nicer hotel further downtown, the Sheraton Center on Seventh Avenue and 52nd Street. There, he buys a copy of *Playboy* magazine, the one with the Lennon interview, and reads it as he eats lunch. He finds the article fascinating, and one particular fact sticks in his mind: *Sometimes they hire fans off the street to work for them.* Wow!

It is the night of December 7, Pearl Harbor Day. Chapman sits in his hotel room, thinking about *The Catcher in the Rye* and his alter ego, Holden Caulfield. The time is growing near. Soon, he will enter the pages of the novel, Chapter 27. But right now, on what might very well be the last night of his life, he's feeling lonely and wants company. *What would Holden do?* He'd have a prostitute come to his room, that's what. It is written. Chapman calls an escort service that he finds in the Yellow Pages. They send over a woman. She's beautiful and she's wearing a green dress, just like Holden's prostitute, Sunny. Synchronicity, the prophecy coming to pass.

He instructs the young woman to take off her green dress and get into bed with him. She does. He then tells her that he doesn't want to do anything—just like Holden. Chapman is confused about sex. Although he takes pleasure in touching and being touched, he doesn't enjoy intercourse.[1]

In the wee hours of the morning of December 8, the day of the Immaculate Conception, the prostitute leaves. Alone again in his hotel room, Chapman opens his Bible to the Gospel According to

---

[1] Jack Jones, *Let Me Take You Down: Inside the Mind of Mark David Chapman, the Man Who Killed John Lennon* (New York: Villard, 1992), p. 16.

John. He changes the title, adding the word "Lennon": *The Gospel According to John Lennon*. He reads from the book, John 14:20: *I am in He, and you in me, and I in you.* The Walrus, indeed. Damn phony can't even write his own lyrics. He steals them from the Bible.

Dawn in New York, a cold December sunrise, order some breakfast from room service. Work to be done. A shrine to be built. Yes, a shrine. *Just to make sure they know who I am.*

The shrine, arranged in a neat semicircle on the desk, includes his passport, for purposes of identification; a Todd Rundgren tape, just so they know he's not a Lennon freak, that Todd is God, and his music, not Lennon's, is the true music of genius; the Bible, open to "The Gospel According to John Lennon"; two snapshots of himself with a group of laughing children from his days working with Vietnamese refugees for the YMCA; and a small poster of Dorothy and the Cowardly Lion from *The Wizard of Oz,* his favorite movie.[2]

Out into the street, loaded pistol concealed in his coat pocket, a recently purchased edition of Lennon's best-selling album *Double Fantasy* under his arm. Today is the day. He can feel it. On Seventh Avenue, in a stationery shop, he buys a copy of *The Catcher in the Rye.* He's been without the book for too long. Opening it to the inside front cover he writes, "This is my statement," and signs it "Holden Caulfield."

He arrives early at the Dakota and parks himself in front, among the troupies, to wait for a sign. Minutes later a sign appears: Mia Farrow and her brood of children. They walk right by Chapman, cross Central Park West, and vanish into the park. The mother of *Rosemary's Baby* herself. Satan's baby, born in the Dakota. Directed by Roman Polanski. His wife, Sharon Tate, murdered by the Manson family, driven to Helter Skelter by the "White Album."

If this is not synchronicity, nothing is.

Chapman waits. The hours pass. And then, late in the afternoon, he sees him—John Lennon emerging from the Dakota with his wife, Yoko Ono, and an entourage, heading for a limousine parked in front of the building on 72nd Street. He knows they're going to the recording studio. But he's not thinking of murder

---

[2] Ibid. p. 19.

now. He's a fan caught in the blinding aura of the superstar he once worshiped. He wants an autograph. He wants Lennon to sign his name on *Double Fantasy*. What a thing to take home to Hawaii and show everybody. Nobody will believe it. Screwing up all his courage, he approaches Lennon, holding out the LP, his tongue completely tied.

Lennon reaches out, takes the album from him.

To Lennon, the young man with the *Double Fantasy* is just another fan. He has no idea that Mark David Chapman has been stalking him for two months.

But Chapman is actually thinking about the *Playboy* interview, and how the Lennons sometimes hire fans off the street. In his deranged mind he figures that he might like to work in the Dakota, and if John hires him, there'll be no need to kill him.

"Is this what you want?" John asks, scrawling his name and the date on the cover.

Mister Lennon, are there any jobs available in your office? It is a triumph of will to get the words out.

Paul Goresh, an amateur photographer who haunts the Dakota,

AP/Wide World Photos

A distraught Yoko Ono, helped by record-company president David Geffen (right), emerges from Roosevelt Hospital in Manhattan just before midnight on December 8, 1980— moments after learning that John Lennon has died.

Julian Lennon (left) and Fred Seaman, John
Lennon's personal assistant, arrive at the
Dakota the night of December 9, 1980. Julian
had just flown in from London to see Yoko
and Sean.

snaps a picture—24 hours later it will be on the front page of *The Daily News*.

"Send in your resume," John suggests to Chapman. He then climbs into the limousine, which speeds off towards Columbus Avenue.

"You really scored," says Goresh, referring to the autographed album.

Chapman offers to buy the picture he just took for fifty dollars. Goresh says he'll have it for him tomorrow.

Chapman continues to stand in front of the Dakota. The sun moves west, sinking behind the Hudson River into New Jersey. As it grows dark and chilly, the fans begin to leave. They'll be back tomorrow. Then, around eight o'clock, Goresh decides to call it a night. Chapman begs him to stay for another picture when the Lennons return. Goresh isn't interested. He can take pictures of the Lennons anytime. He leaves Chapman standing there alone in the darkness.

For the next three hours Chapman keeps his solitary vigil in front of the Dakota. He reads *The Catcher in the Rye* as if he is reading the Bible. It comforts him, gives him the courage he needs to do the job that is before him. He's only doing what Holden would do. If Holden were in his shoes, he'd slaughter the big phony...for the sake of the children.

At 11 P.M. Chapman sees a white limousine pull up in front of the Dakota. He knows who's in there even before he sees them. He knows the moment, the fulfilling of the prophecy, is at hand. Watching from the shadows under the archway, he sees Ono, then Lennon, emerge from the limousine and walk past him into the archway.

"Mister Lennon," Chapman calls out, feeling like a Dakota gargoyle come alive.[3] Crouched in the combat stance, he takes careful aim with his .38-caliber revolver. Then, he pulls the trigger, pumping five hollow-point bullets into John Lennon's back and arm. As the explosions echo under the archway and the bullets tear apart Lennon's insides, Chapman has no identity; he is nobody and nothing—an empty shell committing murder. He may as well be committing suicide, "surrogate suicide," as the psychiatrists will soon say. And then he waits, fully expecting to disappear into the pages of *The Catcher in the Rye*, thereby becoming the Catcher in the Rye for his generation. It says so in Chapter 27, his chapter, the one he has just written in Lennon's blood.

---

[3] Ibid. p. 6.

THE DIAGNOSIS

ACELEBRITY HAS BEEN MURDERED AND PEOPLE NEED to understand why. Is Mark David Chapman insane, or just really pissed off? The world media waits for diagnosis, instant analysis. Nobody has ever assassinated a popular entertainer before. This is completely different, a new kind of madness. It's very scary shit.

First in Bellevue Hospital and later in Riker's Island prison, psychiatrists examine the killer, a young man who has just forged a new identity in blood. He's no longer a loser. He's a famous murderer, an international celebrity. And nobody understands this better than Mark David Chapman himself. Somewhere down the corridor from his cell, a TV is playing. It's time for the evening news. Chapman can hear the resonant, instantly recognizable voice of Walter Cronkite. The venerable anchorman is saying his name, the name that's on everybody's lips, the name that's in boldface type in the gossip columns, where all the important games are played out. **Mark David Chapman.** Bigger than **Lee Harvey Oswald.** If the gossip columns say it, it must be true. That's the way it is.

The psychiatrists come in waves to examine the prisoner. And though they reach strikingly different conclusions about why he shot Lennon five times in the back and arm with hollow-point bullets, they all agree on one point: The famous murderer is a cooperative subject, indeed. He willingly answers all their stupid-ass questions. He wants to be helpful. He wants the doctors to understand what he did. *He* wants to understand what he did.

Doctor Naomi Goldstein, who is on duty at Bellevue early in the morning of December 9, is the first one to examine Chapman. She sees him only hours after the murder. She is the only psychiatrist who interviews him who is not writing a book or working for either the prosecution or defense.[4] To this day she cannot figure out if Chapman is crazy. He had "an insatiable need for attention and recognition," she says simply.[5]

Psychiatrists for the prosecution agree with Goldstein on this one point. Otherwise, they find the patient highly neurotic but quite sane, thank you. He knew just what he was doing. He did it for fame. He killed Lennon to be "important."

Psychiatrists for the defense beg to differ. He's schizophrenic, they say. There's an entire race of "Little People" living in his head. You call this normal? They describe the murder as a "surrogate suicide." By killing John Lennon, Mark David Chapman was killing himself. He killed Lennon to stop his pain, the pain he felt Lennon caused with his "hypocrisy," "phoniness," and ostentatious displays of wealth. It was Chapman's "inner child" who pulled the trigger.

Another team of defense psychiatrists describes a battle between good and evil raging in Chapman's head. Chapman, they say, believed he was possessed by evil spirits who were determined to kill Lennon. He fought with them. Part of him, the good part, wanted nothing more than to go home with the picture of Lennon autographing his *Double Fantasy* album, hang it on his wall and look at it every day. He wanted to lead a normal life and think about what almost happened.

Months later, in Riker's Island, where he is held before trial, Chapman offers an entirely different explanation. "I murdered John Lennon to promote *The Catcher in the Rye*," he says. John Lennon had to die so everybody would read the book. Somehow, Chapman gets a hold of a carton of *Catchers*, and he hands the book out to everybody he meets in jail—guards, prisoners, psychiatrists, journalists. To make sure that they keep it, he autographs each copy, giving it value, transforming it into a macabre collectible, like one of those dolls made from the thread of an unraveled sock that Charlie Manson occasionally sends to people he likes.

On the advice of his court-appointed attorney, Jonathan Marks, Chapman pleads not guilty by reason of insanity to the crime of second-degree murder.

---

[4] Ibid. p. 77.
[5] Ibid. p. 78.

G O D ' S   D E C I S I O N

ON THE DAY OF HIS TRIAL, JUNE 22, 1981, MARK DAVID Chapman has a change of heart. His attorney, Jonathan Marks, tries to talk him out of it, but Chapman will not listen. He wants to plead guilty to murder.

The plea bargaining is done behind closed doors, "to protect the defendant's rights," explains Judge Dennis Edwards. Neither the public nor the press is allowed to witness the hearing. They are forced to wait outside the courtroom. Journalists and fans mill about the corridor, muttering darkly of conspiracies and cover-ups. But the words are said in frustration, without conviction. Everybody has been looking forward to "The Trial of the Century." Now there won't be one.

Edwards, in return for the guilty plea, promises Chapman that his sentence will not exceed 20 years to life. (Had he stood trial, Chapman would have faced a possible sentence of 25 years to life.) The defendant is not concerned with his sentence. He pleaded guilty, he says, because God told him to.

Allen F. Sullivan, an Assistant District Attorney, asks Chapman why he used hollow-point bullets to shoot the ex-Beatle. "To insure Lennon's death," Chapman replies.

"This is your own decision?" Sullivan asks of the guilty plea.

"It is my decision and God's decision."

"When you say it's God's decision...did you hear any voices in your ears?"

"Any audible voices?"

"Any audible voices," Sullivan says.

"No, sir."

"Before you made this decision, did you indulge in any prayer?"

"Yes, there were a number of prayers."

"After you prayed, did you come to the realization that you

understood to come from God that you should plead guilty?"

"Yes, it was his directive, command."

"Is that a realization you came to within yourself, inspired perhaps by God?"

"No, I felt it was God telling me to plead guilty, and then probing with my own decision whether to do what God wanted me to do or whether to do what I wanted to do. I decided to follow God's directive."

"Would you say at this time that this plea is a result of your own free will?"

"Yes."

CHAPTER 27

On the stifling day of August 24, 1981—a Honolulu-like day—about two hundred members of the press and a handful of spectators wait for the famous assassin to be brought before the New York State Supreme Court in downtown Manhattan and sentenced for his crime of second-degree murder. The courtroom is packed, and the energy level is high with anticipation, the kind of anticipation that normally might precede a rock concert. Everybody cranes their necks to get a good look at the manacled star as he is marched into the room wearing a bulletproof vest under a dark blue shirt. He looks sad and pathetic, a pawn in the clutches of something he barely understands. Though there is no longer any need for a trial, there is a primal need for a public shaming, a verbal tarring and feathering before the world media. Everybody knows why Mark David Chapman did it. They've known it for eight months. *He did it for fame.*

And there's certainly a lot of fame up for grabs in the courtroom this day. It would be unfair to suggest that *everyone* there—all the journalists, expert witnesses, lawyers—has the same objective: to be famous. The judge, Dennis Edwards, for example, appears to be utterly benign, a kindly old man, low-key in his demeanor. Indeed, he seems almost bored by what is happening, and so drowsy from the heavy August humidity that he dozes off for a few moments at the bench, but nobody seems to notice, or care. And the defense attorney, Jonathan Marks, carries himself with an air of dignity. He does seem to be concerned that his client be given a fair hearing.

But there appears to be only one difference between Chapman and virtually everybody else who is participating in this hearing: The defendant has far more radical ideas about how far he's willing to go to achieve celebrity. For one grotesque moment, Chapman, a cowardly loser, an empty shell of a human being, managed to manipulate himself into acting with the courage of his monstrous convictions. He has done exactly what he wanted to do; he has transformed himself into the world's most famous antihero.

Consequently, the air is thick with vengeful jealousy. People are furious at Chapman not only because he killed John Lennon, but also because he committed a brutal attack on the status quo, an act of class warfare. John Lennon was a very successful professional, a member of the power elite. And the very successful professionals in this courtroom take it personally. Chapman has stolen John Lennon's fame, and they're not about to let him enjoy it. But the sad fact is that whatever fleeting fame they might be able to grasp this day will depend strictly upon their relationship to the killer. *I psychoanalyzed him. I prosecuted him. I wrote a story about him.*

The expert witnesses have prepared well for their moment in the spotlight, for this merging of the personal and historical. The psychiatrists could be mistaken for actors auditioning for a TV mini-series. If there is fault to be found in their performances, it's that most of them are transparent. They smile too much. They look too happy, too smug, as though they aren't concerned with any antiquated notions of justice, but are thinking instead about book deals.

The psychiatrists for the prosecution repeat what they've been saying since December: Chapman was sane, he knew exactly what he was doing, and *he did it for fame.* The defense psychiatrists, of course, talk of his schizophrenia, the "Little People," his pain.

Apparently, nobody on either side is familiar with Yoko Ono's intriguing statement on reincarnation: "Your brother is the person you murdered in your past life." So nobody has bothered to ask Chapman, *Do you expect to be John Lennon's brother in your next life?*

The Lennon fans add a surreal touch to the proceedings. Many of them are long-haired in that "John '68" style. They wear wire-rimmed glasses and T-shirts with Lennon's image on it. They're outnumbered by reporters by at least two to one, and they're anxious to share their opinions with "the men of the press."

"Mark David Chapman," opines one fan, "was just a cowardly fuck who did it for fame."

"Now he deserves to die," adds another. "And I'd be happy to pull the switch."

Allen Sullivan, the prosecutor, describes Chapman as a man who "has never exhibited any true remorse" and who is "only interested in himself, his own well-being, what affects him, what's important to him at this particular moment." He then proceeds to hammer home the point that Chapman "did it for fame, personal aggrandizement, to draw attention to himself, to massage his own ego. The defendant was concerned throughout that he become famous." His proof: Chapman wanted photographer Paul Goresh, who'd previously photographed Lennon signing Chapman's copy of *Double Fantasy*, to wait until Lennon returned from his recording session so he could get a photo of the murder.

Sullivan makes it sound as if the desire for fame is a shameful thing, a crime in itself. But his words ring hollow. It's an ugly show that intentionally overlooks the one hideous fact that hangs like fog in the courtroom. It is the one fact that nobody dares mention: In America in 1981, particularly in a city like New York, fame is a crucial commodity, and anonymity is a toxic condition that can lead to murderous rage.

Holden Caulfield, or John Lennon for that matter, would have puked.

Before Judge Dennis Edwards passes sentence, Chapman is given the opportunity to speak. But there's little he can do to help himself. Chapman has already pleaded guilty. The evidence against him is overwhelming. There is literally a smoking gun. The verdict may as well have been preordained. He is getting locked up somewhere for the rest of his life. Once, the only real question was if it was going to be in prison or in an institution for the criminally insane. Now there is no question.

Looking like a martyr in a bulletproof vest, he stands up and faces the judge. He has his "Bible" with him—his well-thumbed copy of *The Catcher in the Rye*. "I've chosen this passage as my final spoken words," he vows—a vow he'll soon break. He opens to Chapter 22, in which Holden, after being thrown out of school for failing four subjects, tells his little sister, Phoebe, what he wants to do with his life.

The murderer begins reading. "Anyway, I keep picturing all these little kids playing some game in this big field of rye and all." He's nervous and at first he falters. Then something clicks and he hits his stride, his voice suddenly strong and clear, smooth and flawless. He is well rehearsed, and he does Salinger justice.

"Thousands of little kids and nobody around—nobody big, I mean except me. And, I'm standing on the edge of some scary cliff. What I have to do, I have to catch everybody if they start to go over the cliff—I mean if they're running and they don't look where they're going I have to come out from somewhere and catch them. That's all I'd do all day. I'd just be the catcher in the rye and all."

This is his message and confession. Mark David Chapman is the Catcher in the Rye for his generation; he has murdered John Lennon to save the little children.

Then Chapman tells the hushed courtroom, "I feel like a bloodied prizefighter in the 27th round." These are the exact words he said to a psychiatrist in Hawaii after his suicide attempt. But nobody knows what he's talking about. They understand neither the significance of 27, the triple 9, nor the significance of Chapter 27, the missing chapter of *The Catcher in the Rye,* Chapman's chapter written in Lennon's blood. They are just the meaningless words of a madman, signifying nothing.

The judge then passes sentence and Chapman is taken away still wearing manacles. He walks fearlessly out of the courtroom, holding his head high, veritably glowing with pride. He's done what he came to do.

Afterwards, outside the courtroom, the media, with their pens and floodlights and cameras at the ready, descend upon the expert witnesses for the prosecution, and Sullivan, the prosecutor. They are the winning team. They stand in a tight little knot, preening in the floodlights, everybody smiling broadly, patting each other on the back, congratulating themselves on a job well done. The only thing missing is champagne, which will probably come later, at the private party.

"Was justice served?" the media demands to know.

Of course justice was served. The killer will most likely spend the rest of his life in jail.

Then there is nothing for them to do but go home and watch themselves on the evening news, look at their pictures in the morning newspapers.

Except for Mark David Chapman. He will continue the great

fall described in the dark prophecy in Chapter 24 of *The Catcher in the Rye*. Mr. Antolini, an old teacher of Holden's—another "pervert," actually—tells him, "This fall I think you're riding for—it's a special kind of fall, a horrible kind. The man falling isn't permitted to feel or hear himself hit bottom. He just keeps falling and falling."

Chapman will soon discover what lies at the bottom of the "bottomless" pit: solitary confinement in Attica, possession by demons.

Imagine no possession.

"That kills me." That's what Holden Caulfield would have said, anyway.

DAKOTA:
A FANTASY

NEW YORK CITY, WEDNESDAY, JANUARY 9, 1980, 2:07 P.M.—John Lennon inhaled deeply from his joint of Thai weed, the second of the day, thick enough to be a spliff. Sitting in the "bogus position" on his bed, the quote from *The National Enquirer* stuck in his brain, rattling about, *"If I hadn't made money honestly, I'd have been a criminal. I was just born to be rich."* And his mind reeled backwards through the years. He saw himself in Liverpool, in the Cavern Club, in 1961, leather-clad and sweating, playing to a lunchtime audience, the women shrieking, grabbing at him.

But what if fucking Brian had never walked in? What if it just never bloody happened? Imagine me stuck in Liverpool at 21, going nowhere fast, drinking meself into a fucking stupor every night. I'd be mugging bloody seamen down by the docks for a couple of extra quid. Yeah, right, some fucking genius. I'm lucky I didn't go mad and fucking kill someone. It could have happened. But it didn't and instead I'm doing me time in a gilded prison.

EPILOGUE

AFTERMATH

I N JANUARY 1981, LITTLE MORE THAN A MONTH AFTER John Lennon was gunned down before her eyes, **Yoko Ono** released *Walking on Thin Ice,* the song she and Lennon were working on the night he was murdered. In March, Ono returned to the studio to channel her emotion into *Season of Glass,* an LP hailed by some as an act of artistic bravery and condemned by others as crass exploitation. One song, *No, No, No,* opens on the sound of gunshots. The album cover itself is a photograph of Lennon's bloodstained eyeglasses. It was vintage Yoko: outrageous, confrontational, infuriating, and calculated to provoke controversy—a postmodern demonstration of Oscar Wilde's contention that the only thing worse than being talked about is not being talked about.

In the 22 years since Lennon's death, Ono has kept people talking: by staunchly advocating gun control, by fiercely protecting the John Lennon trademark, and by releasing an avalanche of Lennon's work, notably the *John Lennon Anthology* CD and his book *Skywriting By Word of Mouth.* Ono has also been productive in her own right. A traveling retrospective of her 40-year career as a conceptual artist was accompanied by the release of the book *Yes Yoko Ono,* a critical analysis of that career. Her recent CD's include *Blueprint for a Sunrise, Ono Box,* and—backed by Sean Lennon and his band Ima—*Rising.*

Confounding expectations, Ono continues to live in the Dakota, and until recently was romantically involved with Sam Havadtoy, her former interior decorator. In 2001, after a nearly 30-year separation, Yoko reunited with her daughter Kyoko and discovered she was the grandmother of a boy and a girl.

Sean Lennon was sent to a Swiss boarding school after his father's murder and did not emerge from seclusion until his early

In a rare show of harmony, Yoko Ono, Julian
Lennon, Sean Lennon, and Cynthia Lennon get
together for a drink at New York City's Hard
Rock Cafe to celebrate Julian's concert at
the Beacon Theatre on August 3, 1989.

teens, when he sent gossip columnists into a frenzy by hanging out
with Michael Jackson. After a few semesters at Columbia University,
Sean dropped out to search for himself: he went on tour with the
band Cibo Matto, playing bass and dating the group's leader, key-
boardist Yuka Honda—a Japanese woman several years Sean's sen-
ior who had immigrated to the United States. In 1998, on the eve
of the release of his first CD, *Into the Sun*, an eclectic work of alternative rock, Sean set off a media firestorm worthy of his parents—
he claimed the CIA had assassinated his father. But it was "Come
Together: A Night for John Lennon's Words and Music," broadcast
live from New York in October 2001, that brought to the attention
of a wider audience the fact that Sean, like his conspicuously absent
brother, Julian, sounded a hell of a lot like John Lennon. Wearing
a "Bermuda 80" jersey, a souvenir of the last summer he'd spent

with John, Sean sang *Julia*—John's ode to his own mother—and harmonized with Rufus Wainwright and Moby on *Across the Universe*. Today Sean, who occasionally backs up Yoko Ono's live performances, has his own apartment in New York City and a deal with the Beatles' label, Capitol Records.

In the years immediately following John's death, **Julian Lennon,** living with his mother, Cynthia Twist Lennon, in Ruthin, Wales, was receiving a hundred pounds a week from Yoko Ono. "It was barely enough money to buy beer," Julian has said. Feeling desperate, he lashed out at Ono in the press. "If I were kidnapped, Yoko wouldn't pay the ransom," he told a reporter in 1981. Three years later, Julian, choosing to follow in John's footsteps, left school and became a professional musician. His debut LP, *Valot,* featured a hit single, *Too Late for Goodbyes*. Singing this sad song about his relationship with John, Julian sounded eerily like his father. But his next three albums, *The Secret Value of Daydreaming* (1986), *Mr. Jordan* (1989), and *Help Yourself* (1991), were critical and commercial disasters. As the music business chewed up and spat out Julian, the bitter dispute with Ono over Julian's share of the Lennon legacy continued to fester in the media. Julian expressed disgust over Ono's licensing of his father's image for coffee mugs and other trinkets. Not even his reported $10-million inheritance and a percentage of his father's record royalties put an end to it. In a letter posted on his website on the 20th anniversary of John's death, Julian called his father a "manipulated lost soul" who'd been "sucked into a black hole," and blamed Ono for the breakdown of his relationship with John. He has since used his belated inheritance to form a film company, Pictures From Another Room, which is dedicated to producing films about indigenous tribes, and a music company, Music From Another Room, which in 1998 released his recording *Photograph Smile*. Julian splits his time between an apartment in Monte Carlo and an apartment in Italy, near Lake Como.

Cynthia Twist Lennon, John's first wife, was barely able to make ends meet as she raised Julian alone after her divorce from Lennon. John's death didn't change that. Cynthia inherited nothing, and her financial struggles continued through three failed marriages.

She was an unhappy reminder that the Lennon name guaranteed nothing in the way of fortune or success. But through it all she remained close to Julian and now resides in a beachfront cottage near Cherbourg, France, pursuing the painting career she'd put aside when she married John.

Until she died in December 1991 at age 85, John Lennon's aunt, **Mimi Smith,** lived quietly in Poole, Dorset, in the seaside bungalow John had bought her in 1965.

May Pang's memoir about her relationship with John Lennon, *Loving John* (later retitled *John Lennon: The Lost Weekend*), was published in 1983. Like so many people who were involved with Lennon, John's spirit seemed to hover over her through a marriage, two children, and a separation. She will always be known as John Lennon's former mistress, and she coexists happily with his ghost, occasionally giving "Remembering John" seminars. A music manager, Pang lives in Pomona, New York, and is a devotee of feng shui, the ancient Chinese art of harmonious placement. She maintains a website, www.maypang.com.

John Green, a.k.a. **Charlie Swan**, may have been a talented psychic, but he failed to foresee the impending tragedy of December 8, 1980, a lapse that contributed to the termination of his employment with Yoko Ono. Green then wrote *Dakota Days*, a memoir about his experiences with the Lennons, which was published in 1983. Though an entertaining and in many ways an insightful book, its credibility is marred by Green's penchant for taking full credit for everything that went right with the Lennons and absolving himself of all blame for anything that went wrong. He lives in Washington, D.C., and remains a professional tarot-card reader, astrologer, and writer, though one who keeps a very low profile.

Elliot Mintz, a master of disseminating disinformation to the media—implying, for example, that the biography I was to write with Fred Seaman was a CIA/FBI-based attempt to destroy John Lennon's reputation—was promoted to official spokesman for Yoko Ono in the aftermath of John Lennon's assassination. Happiness was the cool revolver he began to carry in his shoulder holster. Any time Mintz imagined an enemy behind a door, it gave him pleasure, especially if people were watching, to draw the gun and show off his James-Bond–like moves. The pistol was a necessity, he said—there were conspiracies afoot, and Mintz needed to defend himself, Yoko, and Sean ("Carol and the baby," as he called them in public) from predators, both domestic and foreign. His unwavering devotion to Ono was rewarded in 1988, when she allowed him to be the narrator of *The Lost Lennon Tapes*, a radio broadcast famous for spawning a multitude of bootlegs. Though he continues to focus the lion's share of his attention on managing Ono's media relations, Mintz now counts Bob Dylan and Don Johnson among his stable of superstar clients.

David Geffen rushed to Roosevelt Hospital to be with Yoko Ono when he learned that John Lennon had been shot. By the time he arrived, Lennon was already dead. He escorted a devastated Ono from the hospital and then issued a brief statement: "John loved and prayed for the human race. Please do the same for him." Though Geffen's grief was undoubtedly sincere, it was impossible to ignore the effect Lennon's death had on Geffen Records—it sent *Double Fantasy* straight to number one, and the album just kept selling, transforming the fledgling company into a major player in the music business. Geffen, with an infallible eye for talent, would go on in the 1980's to sign such acts as Aerosmith, Guns N' Roses, and Nirvana. The sale of the company to MCA in 1990 netted Geffen $710 million and a reputation as Hollywood's first self-made billionaire. With his newfound wealth, Geffen, along with Steven Spielberg and Jeffrey Katzenberg, founded DreamWorks SKG, a multimedia entertainment company. Since its inception in 1994, the DreamWorks film studio—the first Hollywood studio built in 60 years—has released a string of Academy Award winners: *Saving Private Ryan*, *American Beauty, Gladiator, Shrek,* and *A Beautiful Mind.*

Geffen, who provided financial backing to Bill Clinton's presidential campaign, has also contributed hundreds of millions of dollars to such organizations as AIDS Project Los Angeles and the Gay Men's Health Crisis. Yet, until he came out publicly as a gay man in 1992, he was subject to bitter attacks for his "dishonesty." Today, he remains one of the most controversial people in the entertainment business, perceived as both a vindictive bully prone to irrational screaming fits and a devoted friend admired for his astounding generosity.

Double Fantasy producer **Jack Douglas**, who'd once written songs for Robert Kennedy's senate campaign, was one of the last people to see John Lennon alive. Lennon and Ono were working with Douglas the night of December 8, 1980, putting the finishing touches on Ono's *Walking on Thin Ice*. The murder left Douglas despondent, but he tried to lose himself in his work; he produced The Knack and Graham Parker. Two years later, there was another nasty bit of business to deal with: Ono refused to pay Douglas royalties owed on *Double Fantasy*. He was forced to sue. At the trial, Douglas has said, Ono's psychics and witches were in the courtroom, "trying to put a spell" on him. But he won the case. Douglas continues to produce records for some of the top acts in rock 'n' roll, including Aerosmith, and considers himself very lucky for having had the opportunity to work with John Lennon.

The years after John Lennon's murder were difficult for actor **Peter Boyle**. Roles were few and far between; there was nothing until 1984, when he played opposite Michael Keaton in *Johnny Dangerously*. In 1990 a mild stroke knocked him out of action for another four years. He returned to acting with roles in the films *The Santa Clause* and *While You Were Sleeping* and on the TV shows *NYPD Blue* and *The X-Files,* for which he won an Emmy. Now, having achieved prime-time recognition as Ray Romano's father on the hit TV sitcom *Everybody Loves Raymond* and having garnered critical praise for his role as a racist father—echoes of *Joe*—in the film *Monster's Ball,* Boyle is enjoying the prime of his career. Still married to Lorraine Alterman (she'd introduced him to Lennon, who was the best man at their wedding), Boyle continues to live in Manhattan. Despite the abusive Palm Beach incident, Boyle, who spent a short time as a monk in the Christian Brothers order, has never publicly said a harsh word about Lennon.

Though their stormy relationship was at a low ebb in 1980, John Lennon's murder devastated **Paul McCartney**. It meant he'd never be able to resolve his differences with a man he'd always thought of as a friend and a brother. It also ended his dream of a Beatles reunion, and nobody wanted that more than Paul. Yet Lennon's subsequent canonization spurred McCartney to new heights of musical mass production. His output since 1980 is unparalleled, his numbers Ruthian. The only records he has left to break are his own. You can look it up—in *The Guinness Book of World Records*. But pop music is only the tip of the McCartney iceberg. Paul, it appeared, was determined to prove that he, not John, was the most talented Beatle, the greatest artist. An authorized biography, *Paul McCartney: Many Years from Now* by Barry Miles, described McCartney as the one who filled Lennon's head with avant-garde ideas and who was busy pioneering the Beatles' experimental music while John sat around getting stoned in the suburbs.

McCartney became a Renaissance man for the Age of Disposable Culture. He got into everything: classical music, filmmaking, painting, poetry. An abbreviated cataloguing of the works he has created since Lennon's death only hints at the compulsion.

There were solo record albums; there were Wings albums; there were *Beatles Anthology* albums; there was a Beatles greatest-hits album; there were full-length classical works; there were films; there were books; there were tours; and there were public appearances. Taken together, it's a portrait of a man whose only fear is being out of the spotlight, a man in a perpetual state of spewing *something*. Because of his profound impact on the British economy, Queen Elizabeth knighted him in 1994, making him Sir Paul.

In April 1998, his wife of 29 years, Linda McCartney—the mother of their children, Mary, Stella, James and Heather (Paul's stepdaughter)—died of breast cancer, the disease that had killed Paul's mother. To honor Linda's memory, Paul embarked on a series of campaigns in defense of animal rights. At a Waldorf-Astoria ceremony two years later, he inducted John Lennon into the Rock 'n' Roll Hall of Fame. In July 2001, he announced his engagement to Heather Mills, a model who'd lost a leg in a traffic accident, and together they launched a crusade against land mines. Almost a year later—one week before his 60th birthday—Paul and Heather were married in an Irish castle. The message, like the song, was clear: Life goes on....

And then there was **Ringo**, "Young Ringo," the oldest Beatle, so sickly as a child that he almost didn't survive. Ringo Starr, the one John Lennon, at the height of the madness, used to look at to remind himself the Beatles were human. Easygoing Ringo, the one who stayed friends with John when it was over, the last Beatle to see Lennon alive. In the aftermath of the murder, Ringo released a record, the dismal *Stop and Smell the Roses,* the LP Lennon was supposed to contribute to. It failed, and then Ringo, the Human Metronome with the delightful voice, lost his record deal and turned to alcohol and cocaine. In and out of rehab, he managed to hold on to one gig: hosting a weekly radio show, *Ringo's Yellow Submarine.* "They want him to tap-dance in Newcastle," said Neil Aspinall, managing director of Apple Corps, who remained close to the surviving Beatles. "But Ringo's too strong. He'll never tap-dance in Newcastle."

It took the better part of the decade for Ringo to sober up. The birth of Tatia Jayne, the daughter of his oldest son Zak (and the first Beatle grandchild), probably helped. Considering Ringo's predilection for liquor, the Sun Country Wine Cooler commercial two years later, in 1987, was perhaps not the best career move. Still, it was historic: he was the first (and so far remains the only) Beatle to peddle a product on TV. Then came the children's television series *Shining Time Station;* Ringo played "Mr. Conductor."

It wasn't until 1989 that Ringo returned to doing what he did best: playing music live, onstage. Ringo and his All Starr Band went on tour. A live album followed, and in 1998 a studio album, *Vertical Man.* But even through the good times there were plenty of reminders that ex-Beatles are not immune to life's quotidian horrors. Ringo's first wife, Maureen Cox—with whom Ringo had remained friendly—died from cancer in 1994, and a few years later their 24-year-old daughter Lee was hospitalized with a brain tumor. Still, Ringo and his wife, Barbara Bach, managed to enjoy life, shuttling between their homes in Monte Carlo, Los Angeles and Colorado. Ringo transformed himself into the corporate man, a star of multiple TV commercials, selling far more sobering products than wine cooler for the companies Discover Card, Pizza Hut, Century 21, and, memorably, Charles Schwab. Very lucrative. Very hip. Very funny. And it wasn't tap-dancing in Newcastle.

George Harrison, who had feared for his safety since the days of Beatlemania, felt even more vulnerable after John Lennon's murder. He was also haunted by the knowledge that he'd never reconcile with Lennon, who hadn't spoken to him in years. Harrison sought solace in his music, releasing two albums: *Somewhere in England* in 1981, highlighted by *All Those Years Ago,* a Lennon tribute recorded with Paul and Ringo, and *Gone Troppo* in 1982, an LP best forgotten. George then became "The Hermit of Friar Park," locking himself away at his estate at Henley-on-Thames for five years of silence and seclusion.

The release of *Cloud Nine* in 1987, which featured his biggest post-Beatle hit, *I've Got My Mind Set on You,* and another Beatles tribute, *When We Was Fab,* marked his return to the material world. A flurry of activity followed. Harrison appeared at New York's Waldorf-Astoria with Ringo, Sean Lennon, Julian Lennon, and Yoko the night in 1988 that Mick Jagger inducted The Beatles into the Rock 'n' Roll Hall of Fame; he jammed onstage with Jagger, Ringo and Bob Dylan. Not long after, he ran off to join the Traveling Wilburys, an "anonymous" supergroup that included Dylan, Tom Petty, Roy Orbison and Jeff Lynne. The Wilburys had one top-ten smash, *Handle With Care.* Re-energized, Harrison toured Japan in 1991 with a band that included Eric Clapton; he began work with the surviving Beatles on the various *Anthology* projects; he attended Grand Prix and motorcycle-racing events; and he secured his reputation as "the cranky one" by trashing Liam Gallagher of Oasis as "silly," Bono of U2 as "egocentric," and rap and techno music as "pollution."

It was in 1997, while gardening at Friar Park, that George, once a heavy smoker, discovered a lump in his throat. He was diagnosed with cancer, which later spread to his lungs. Harrison, determined to live, traveled the world—Switzerland, New York, Minnesota's Mayo Clinic—seeking the best medical care, the most advanced treatments. In the midst of it, he survived a near-fatal knife attack in December 1999 by a madman who'd breached security in Friar Park. In 2000, he released a 30th anniversary edition of *All Things Must Pass,* his first post-Beatle LP, and promoted it with a live Yahoo chat, the first time he'd ever used a computer. By 2001, even though the cancer had spread to his brain, Harrison, in his home recording studio, poured his remaining energy into an album, tentatively titled *Portrait of a Leg-End*, a reference to the leg in the opening credits of *Monty Python's Flying Circus*. His last recording, *Horse to Water*, co-written with his son Dhani, appeared on *Jools Holland Big Band Rhythm and Blues;* RIP Music is credited as publisher. In his final days, Harrison made peace with his estranged sister, Louise, and said goodbye to Paul, Ringo, and his lifelong friend Ravi Shankar, who introduced him to Indian music and the sitar. On November 29, 2001, in Los Angeles, surrounded by Olivia Arias, his wife of 23 years, Dhani, and two chanting Hari Krishnas, George Harrison, age 58, the youngest and most private Beatle, succumbed to cancer.

Denied parole in 2000, **Mark David Chapman** continues to serve his term of 20 years to life in New York's Attica State Prison.

STRAWBERRY FIELDS FOREVER

SOME PEOPLE COME TO STRAWBERRY FIELDS, THE tear-shaped plot of ground in Central Park across the street from the Dakota, only on December 8. Under the scrutiny of the media, they gather in a magic circle around the "Imagine" mosaic, as if performing a séance. Candles burn, musicians play, and a thousand voices sing **John Lennon**'s songs as they try to conjure his spirit. And they do conjure something, but it's not exactly a ghost. It's an energy, a feeling—sadness and love and a longing for what could have been.

What could have been? A lot more good music, for sure. And maybe a voice to say "Stop the madness!" as the madness began to look apocalyptic.

On the night of this horrible anniversary, the Lennon energy is always at its strongest. But you can feel it every other day of the year, too, as fans, drawn by John and his music, come from all over the planet—a phenomenon echoed by a plaque listing 121 countries, from Afghanistan to Zimbabwe, that recognize Strawberry Fields as a garden of peace—to silently gather around the "Imagine" mosaic. Men and women into their 60's and 70's, their grandchildren, and people every age in between remember or imagine. They light candles, they leave bouquets, and they write notes: *Dear John, thanks for 1968. I miss you....*

Marcel Miller

NOTES

I wrote the original "Prelude," first published in June 2000, without the aid of my diaries. Since then, my diaries have been returned to me. Using them, I've made numerous additions and revisions to this edition of the book. The additional diary excerpts are self-evident, the revisions less so. I'd like to point out that in the first sentence of the original text I wrote that Fred Seaman came to my apartment 24 hours after Lennon's murder. I now know that Seaman called me within 24 hours, but came to my apartment five days later.

All dollar figures are in 1980 dollars. One 1980 dollar is worth approximately two dollars in the present day.

SOURCES

Though I believe that most of Albert Goldman's *The Lives of John Lennon* (New York: William Morrow, 1988) is grossly exaggerated, the book was especially useful for names. It's also the only book that succinctly explains the complex lawsuit involving Lennon's *Rock 'n' Roll* album and Morris Levy.

The Last Days of John Lennon (Secaucus, NJ: Birch Lane Press, 1991), by Fred Seaman, was helpful in recreating the atmosphere of 1979-1980, as well as with the chronology of 1980.

Lennon (New York: Harper Perennial, 1992), by Ray Coleman, though sterilized, is the most comprehensive Lennon biography available and the only book that acknowledges Lennon's trip to South Africa.

Dakota Days (New York: St. Martin's Press, 1983), by John Green, the Lennons' tarot-card reader, offers much detail and insight into the Lennons' relationship with the occult.

I've quoted extensively from *Cheiro's Book of Numbers* (Los Angeles: The London Publishing Company, 1929), a classic work of the occult, long out of print in the United States.

Yoko Ono (New York: Macmillan, 1986), by Jerry Hopkins, is the most comprehensive biography of Ono available and was helpful with chronology and details about Ono's background.

Loving John (New York: Warner Books, 1983), by May Pang, gives a sense of the joy Lennon took in his relationship with his former assistant.

Let Me Take You Down: Inside the Mind of Mark David Chapman, the Man Who Killed John Lennon (New York: Villard, 1992), by Jack Jones, is the definitive Mark David Chapman biography and a source of vital information for parts of "The Coda." As indicated in the footnotes, I've paraphrased or quoted from five sentences in this work.

The following books, magazines, newspapers, wire service, and Usenet group were also invaluable sources of information as well as inspiration:

The Catcher in the Rye (New York: Little Brown & Company, 1951) by J.D. Salinger
Skywriting by Word of Mouth (New York: Harper Collins, 1986) by John Lennon
Fear and Loathing in Las Vegas (New York: Random House, 1971) by Hunter S. Thompson

Playboy
Esquire
Town and Country

The New York Post
The New York Times
The Palm Beach Post
The National Enquirer
The Globe

United Press International

Recreation Music Beatles (rec.music.beatles)

INDEX

Please note that photographs are indicated by bold page numbers.